Social Justice
Reconsidered

Social Justice Reconsidered

The Problem of Appropriate Precision in a Theory of Justice

David Mapel

UNIVERSITY OF ILLINOIS PRESS
Urbana and Chicago

© 1989 by the Board of Trustees of the University of Illinois
Manufactured in the United States of America
C 5 4 3 2 1

This book is printed on acid-free paper.

Library of Congress Cataloging-in-Publication Data

Mapel, David, 1952-
 Social justice reconsidered : the problem of appropriate
precision in a theory of justice / David Mapel.
   p.   cm.
 Includes bibliographies and index.
 ISBN 0-252-01598-3 (alk. paper)
 1. Justice. 2. Social justice. I. Title.
JC578.M33 1989
320'.01'1—dc19   88-30131
                                                 CIP

For my mother and father

Contents

Acknowledgments

Special thanks are due to Bryan Barnett, who encouraged and helped me at several stages in writing this book, and to Richard Flathman and Timothy Fuller, who have been exemplary teachers and friends. For their helpful criticism and support I would like to thank Benjamin Barber, Tom Eagles, Horst Mewes, Dennis Eckart, Walt Stone, Jackie Colby, Clelia Demoraes, Cathy Barnett, and especially David Hendrickson and Bonnie Honig. A number of valuable suggestions were also made by the scholar who read the manuscript for the University of Illinois Press. Needless to say, any errors that remain are Hendrickson's alone.

We must be content, then, in speaking of such subjects and with such premises to indicate the truth roughly and in outline, and in speaking about things which are only for the most part true and with premises of the same kind to reach conclusions that are no better. In the same spirit, therefore, should each type of statement be received; for it is the mark of an educated man to look for precision in each class of things just so far as the nature of the subject admits.

Aristotle, *Nichomachean Ethics*

CHAPTER 1

Introduction

The Question of Appropriate Precision in a Theory of Justice

The problem of 'social justice' has been at the center of Anglo-American political philosophy ever since the publication of John Rawls's *A Theory of Justice* (1971). For most of this period, political philosophers have responded to Rawls's work in kind, turning out one "theory of justice" after another, each more abstract, intricate, and hypothetical than the last. But fashions change: theorists like Michael Sandel and Michael Walzer now argue that Rawls and his imitators have been far too ambitious in their attempts to provide a systematic account of social justice. The result, they say, has been a literature that is sterile, apolitical, and academic in the worst sense of the word. Of course, this attack has provoked in turn a defense of Rawls's style of philosophizing and a lively, if somewhat unfocused, debate. This book is about the core of that debate: how much precision *should* we expect in theorizing about social justice?

To illustrate the importance of this question, compare the approaches of two prominent theorists of social justice, Ronald Dworkin and Michael Walzer. Dworkin's writings on equality represent one extreme with respect to the sort of precision that might be demanded from first principles. He aims at nothing less than a description of what complete equality between each member of society would look like, taking into account the resources that each person might possess, the effects of each person's decisions and actions on the holdings of all others over their entire lifetimes, and compensating individuals for the accidents of social background and natural endowment. To describe perfect equality between individuals, Dworkin proposes a counterfactual thought-experiment that employs the device of a hypothetical auction of resources.[1] He then tries to show, in a series of steps, how we might approximate the results of such an auction in practice. As he himself notes, this project reflects a certain style that has recently gripped much of Anglo-American philosophy. It is a style replete with "Mathematical preference functions, fictitious social contracts, and the other paraphernalia of modern political theory."² In short, it is a style that aims at very precise judgments about what is due each member of society.

At the other extreme, Walzer's theory begins with the very Aristotelian idea that distributive justice is concerned with a great variety of goods, each of which can affect people in a great variety of ways. According to Aristotle, this variety gives rise to a great "fluctuation of opinion" about distributive justice. But Walzer here draws the very conclusion that Aristotle warned against: justice is *entirely* a matter of "opinion," or social convention. Beginning with this thoroughgoing moral relativism, Walzer presents a 'pluralistic' theory of justice. He argues that in our society there is an irreducible plurality of first principles of justice, which stand in no fixed relationship to one another. When commonsense principles of need and desert conflict, for example, there is no more fundamental principle, such as Dworkin's principle of "complex equality," to tell us what to do. Not only are there no higher-order standards to which we can appeal when considerations of justice conflict, but in principle *there cannot be.* Philosophy cannot provide a systematic account of social justice even at the most general level, much less determine the overall share of resources that any specific member of society ought to have at any given time. The precision that Walzer expects from a theory of justice is minimal.

An exchange between Dworkin and Walzer in the *New York Review of Books* illustrates what is wrong with the way discussions of this question have generally been conducted. Because the central issue of appropriate precision is nowhere addressed directly, the exchange involves little more than a continual reassertion of opposing points of view without any noticeable progress. Walzer relies on "commonsense" principles of justice; Dworkin tries to devise an account that transcends common sense almost completely. Walzer represents himself as a champion of the claims of "politics" against philosophy; Dworkin sees himself as defending philosophy against "all the impulses that drag us back into our own culture."³

Although Dworkin makes numerous criticisms of Walzer, fundamentally his complaint is that Walzer's theory fails to provide definite enough standards for distributing scarce resources, hence the theory is unacceptable: "Walzer's book provides a wholly unintended defense of the style of philosophy he wants to banish. His failure confirms the instinct that drives philosophers to their formulas and artificial examples and personal intuitions."⁴ This criticism holds only if we have some reason to believe that it is possible to replace commonsense principles with something more precise. Yet this is just what Walzer denies. The limitations of his account, he says, are merely the limitations inherent in any theory that tries to remain true to the complexity of our moral experience. Therefore, by his lights Dworkin is guilty of an arid rationalism. According to Walzer, "the hard task is to find principles latent in the lives of people Dworkin and I live with, principles they can recognize and adopt."[5] Of course, the charge of rationalism against Dworkin is persuasive only if it can be shown just how and why Dworkin's much more precise theory of justice must fail, a task nowhere undertaken by Walzer.

We are left with a protracted discussion in which each party merely presupposes his own answer to the underlying question at hand, because the question is never explicitly recognized or treated on its own. Progress in philosophical discussion has foundered and stalled because of the failure of the participants to grasp and face squarely the central issue between them. At stake here are two very different conceptions of the philosophical enterprise; indeed, perhaps more than two views, since Dworkin and Walzer represent only the most radical positions on this issue. To determine how much precision it is reasonable to expect from a theory of justice is, therefore, both the key to understanding the development of the current debate over theories of social justice and the key to any further progress. My task is to show that it is possible to ask and to answer directly the question of what degree of precision is reasonably possible in a theory of social justice. And while I cannot claim to provide a definitive answer, my aim is to chart the course that must be followed in approaching this critical question.

The Strategy of the Argument

I want to avoid the sort of question begging that is characteristic of much of the current debate over social justice, so I have taken my cue from John Rawls, because no other theorist has devoted half so much attention to the problem of appropriate precision. That problem has been one of the central preoccupations of Rawls's long philosophical career, as the ideas of "pure procedural justice," "representative social positions," "primary goods," "the basic structure," and, most recently, "Kantian constructivism" all attest. In *A Theory of Justice*, Rawls already anticipated and rejected several ways of approaching the problem of social justice that have since reappeared. If he was correct in rejecting those alternatives, his own efforts are significant in a way that has not been generally appreciated.

Perhaps the failure of subsequent theories of justice is merely good evidence of the soundness of Rawls's initial reading of the problem. If so, his own way of posing the problem looks much more like a test case for the possibility of a systematic theory itself, and I will argue that Rawls's work in fact has just this kind of significance. This should not seem surprising, for significant work in philosophy often has more to do with showing what it takes to solve a problem than with actually solving it.

I wish to stress that the focus of my argument is Rawls's understanding of the problems involved in achieving the degree of precision that a theory of justice requires, not his solution to those problems. This understanding is contained in two major claims that must be evaluated. The first claim is that we must take the main institutions of society, or what Rawls calls "the basic structure," as the primary subject of justice. If we do not, we shall either ignore the importance of "background justice" or else have to cope with the unworkable complexities of trying to establish social justice on a case by case basis. This is essentially a claim about the proper "unit of analysis" for a theory of justice.

Rawls's second claim is that we can make the problem of balancing first principles more tractable by incorporating the idea of the basic structure within a more general method of justification. That method, he argues, allows us to make certain simplifications and practical adjustments in the way we pose the problem of justice from the outset, in order to arrive at a determinate viewpoint for assessing the justice of the basic structure as a whole.

The Difficulty of Focusing on Individual Shares
In the next chapter, I will begin to explore the problem of appropriate precision by considering the difficulties involved in using personal desert as a basic principle of social justice. In discussing this subject, critics have usually attacked Rawls's view that the bases of personal desert are themselves undeserved and therefore 'arbitrary from a moral point of view.' I will argue that Rawls can acknowledge that individuals are in principle capable of desert yet rely on some rather standard libertarian arguments to show why desert must nevertheless be subordinated to more fundamental considerations.

Libertarians such as Friedrich A. Hayek have long argued that the market and other institutions of the basic structure prevent us from accurately establishing the value of the contributions that individuals make to society as a whole. They also argue that we cannot use the idea of personal desert to establish the institutional context within which individuals first become deserving. Rawls concurs: "We cannot judge a distribution in isolation from the system of which it is the outcome. If it is asked in the abstract whether one distribution of a given stock of things to definite individuals with known desires and preferences is better than another, then there is simply no answer to this question."[6] On this basis, Hayek and other conservative skeptics have concluded that the idea of personal desert, and indeed the entire notion of social justice, is a meaningless one. Rawls concludes that if the idea of social justice is to be given any intelligible meaning, we must focus on institutions themselves, not on individual claims of merit or equality. On this view, social justice cannot be interpreted as primarily a matter of establishing individual shares and therefore is not primarily a matter of personal desert, complete substantive equality, or any other "individualized" principle of distribution.

Over the last ten years, a number of theories of justice have been proposed that claim to accomplish the very task that Rawls, Hayek, and others have deemed impossible. Theorists have tried to overcome the difficulties involved in focusing on the specific claims of individuals by giving an account of the "overall" set of holdings that individuals are entitled to as a matter of perfect, hypothetical justice. Of course, when Rawls rejected the idea of making general comparisons of each person's overall situation, he could not have foreseen these more recent efforts in any detail. Nor in the interim, unfortunately, has Rawls supported his general rejection of this approach by directly criticizing other recent theories. Since this is by far the most common sort of theory that has recently been put forward, I examine Rawls's first, general claim by focusing on the alternative proposals of three different writers: Ronald Dworkin, Bruce Ackerman, and William Galston. Although these theorists give quite different substantive accounts of justice, each employs a general approach to social justice that Rawls believes cannot lead to workable results. By analyzing the work of these theorists (Chapters 3-5) I will try to show that Rawls's rejection of the idea of focusing on the overall claims of specific individuals is well founded. My argument, in brief, is as follows.

Without too much oversimplification, each of the theorists mentioned can be understood as proposing that the basic principle of social justice should be what Rawls has called "the principle of redress." This principle holds that society should compensate individuals for the accidents of social or natural endowment (or both) on a case by case basis. In contrast, Rawls rejects the principle of redress as a fundamental principle of social justice. As he repeatedly points out, justice as fairness expresses only a "tendency towards equality." According to Rawls,

> it is clear that nothing depends upon being able to identify the initial arrangement [of equality]; indeed, how well-off men are in this situation plays no essential role in applying the difference principle. We simply

maximize the expectations of the least-favored subject to the required constraints. As long as doing this is an improvement for everyone, as we assume it is, the estimated gains from the situation of hypothetical equality are irrelevant, if not largely impossible to ascertain anyway.[7]

In other words, we cannot explain the idea of social justice by comparing the actual holdings of specific individuals against some ideal pattern of holdings that would exist in a more just world. There simply is no absolute starting point or baseline of this sort for measuring departures from what justice ideally requires. Or, as Rawls explains, "Indeed, no sense can be made of the notion of that part of an individual's holdings that exceed what would have been their situation in another society or in a state of nature."[8]

To show that Rawls's assessment of the difficulties involved in focusing directly on individual claims of redress is well founded, I will concentrate primarily on the metrics that have been proposed for commensurating individual claims to "overall equality," as that notion has been variously understood by Dworkin, Ackerman, and others. Because the principle of redress aims at restoring individuals to a situation of equality, it requires a metric of equality. The question of a workable metric is central, because if no feasible measure of overall equality can be found, this negative result will support Rawls's view that the task of selecting specific distributions of desired things must be regarded as mistaken in principle, and in any case not capable of a definite answer.

Several proposed metrics of equality are either senseless or unworkable. A metric is senseless if it relies on imaginary calculations that are impossible or if it fails to identify any common currency by which the relative value of different sorts of resources might be commensurated. A metric is unworkable if it requires information that is too complex and counterfactual to lead to practical principles. As Rawls observes,

> The rules applying to agreements are, after all, practical and public directives, and not mathematical preference functions which may be as complicated as one could wish. Thus any sensible scheme of rules will not exceed the capacity of individuals to grasp and follow them with sufficient ease, nor will it burden citizens with requirements of knowledge and foresight that they cannot possibly meet.[9]

The metrics of overall equality proposed by Dworkin and Galston are, by and large, senseless. Although many critics have drawn this conclusion about Ackerman's notion of "initial equality," this idea is coherent, at least given the assumptions of what Ackerman calls "ideal theory." In practical terms, however, I believe that Ackerman's account of justice turns out to be completely unworkable.

Although the conclusions reached are negative, my examination of these theories is important for two reasons. First, the sophistication of these theories make them ideal foils for an examination of Rawls's approach. Dworkin's theory, in particular, is designed to show that Rawls is wrong about the practical and conceptual impossibility of trying to determine what each particular member of society is due. Second, an examination of these theories brings us full circle. Dworkin anticipates many of the problems involved in commensurating individual claims to scarce resources, although he fails to solve those problems. In principle, Ackerman does solve the problem of a fair "initial" distribution of resources to particular individuals, but he cannot apply his ideal solution to actual circumstances. Galston begins with a theory of the good that allows him to commensurate actual claims on resources once those resources have first been distributed, but his solution to the problem of an initial distribution of economic resources brings back all of the difficulties that Dworkin's theory was designed to solve. In examining these three theories, then, we canvas the full range of problems that are involved in trying to make, in Dworkin's words, "overall comparisons of [each person's] overall situation."[10]

An Alternative to Philosophical Pluralism

Walzer's approach (the balancing of a plurality of first principles by resort to intuition) raises possibly intractable problems of priority between competing principles. Rawls's solution to this problem is to leave the balancing of commonsense precepts to the operation of institutions. For example, the precept "to each according to one's contribution" is weighted in practice by the institution of the market, which controls the supply of labor. The way in which we constrain the market, by conditions of fair equality of opportunity for example, indirectly determines the weight this precept receives relative to other considerations. But institutions like the market must be regulated in terms of the general ends of social policy, such as full employment and greater allocative efficiency. And these social ends, in turn, must somehow be balanced, usually by reference to philosophical first principles such as the principles of utility and equality in the distribution of satisfaction. Thus, focusing on the basic structure by itself does not resolve the problem of pluralism but only transfers it to a higher level of abstraction. But, as Rawls points out, we now encounter a new problem. Philosophical first principles are too comprehensive and abstract for us to have any confidence in our ability to balance them correctly or even to interpret them. For this reason Rawls argues that we must employ a novel method of justification that allows us to simplify the problem of a just basic structure in order to make such balancing problems more manageable.[11]

My discussion of Rawls's second claim (that we must employ a novel method of justification) begins in Chapter 5, where discussion of Galston's theory illustrates the kind of difficulties that arise when we reject Rawls's approach and instead try to elevate several commonsense precepts to the level of first principles. I also consider the more general idea of a "distribution-sensitive consequentialism," as proposed by Galston, Samuel Scheffler, and T. M. Scanlon. The idea behind this type of theory is to treat various kinds of equality and fairness as outcomes, or "states of affairs," which can be combined with various levels of aggregate welfare in order to yield rankings of total "states of affairs," thereby providing yet another way of handling the problem of balancing first principles. I want to show that "distribution-sensitive consequentialism" offers no real alternative to a plurality of first principles, even though it is the only alternative to Rawls's solution.

In Chapter 6, I turn to Rawls's theory itself. My major concern, however, is not *A Theory of Justice* but the revisions to justice as fairness that have been made by some of Rawls's followers, such as Amy Gutmann, and by Rawls himself. It should be noted that there is a significant difference between Rawls and his followers in this regard. Most of the revisions that have been proposed are designed to make justice as fairness more sensitive to the claims of specific individuals. But Rawls believes that these revisions merely reintroduce the unguided balancing problems that his original theory tried to avoid. His own revisions of his theory are more complex: he postpones the problem of constructing an index of primary goods until later in the development of the theory, reconstructs his overall argument in terms of a particular conception of moral personality (to make his derivation of first principles more defensible), and ultimately relies on an empirical "theory of institutions" to show that the outcomes generated by his first principles fall within "an acceptable range."

I do not believe that these adjustments ultimately succeed. For example, Rawls has still not solved the problem of "indexing" the share of primary goods enjoyed by the least-advantaged member of society, even though this is a much simpler problem than trying to devise a metric for individually appraising the situation of each and every member of society. The larger point of Chapter 6, however, is that only by focusing on the basic structure as Rawls does can we avoid the complexities involved in commensurating individual claims and balancing general aggregative and distributive considerations. Moreover, the ultimate failure of Rawls's strategy of focusing on the basic structure shows that we cannot expect much precision either at the level of individual claims or at the level of first principles. Rawls clearly understands why the philosophical alternatives to his theory are unlikely to solve either of these problems, which explains the shape that his theory takes from the beginning. By showing that he correctly appraises the way alternative theories pose the problem of social justice, I try to provide an argument about the sort of precision that we can reasonably expect from a theory of social justice that is quite general in scope.

Reconsidering Commonsense Pluralism

If the sort of theory offered by Dworkin and others is too complex, and if Rawls's theory oversimplifies the problem of social justice, what are the alternatives? The collapse of both Rawls's account and recent alternative theories of justice brings us back, finally, to commonsense pluralism. Although pluralism has been put forward elsewhere, there are several reasons for thinking that it needs a better defense than it has received thus far. First, pluralists have often failed to engage the substantive alternatives offered by their critics, as illustrated by the exchange noted earlier, something I hope to correct in this volume. Second, since I focus on the difficulties inherent in different conceptions of the primary subject of social justice, I must also consider Walzer's view that we should focus on discrete distributive contexts or 'spheres' of justice as our primary subject rather than on the overall claims of specific individuals or the basic structure as a whole. Although this view avoids many of the problems that arise for other approaches to theorizing about social justice, it too has difficulties that must be acknowledged and assessed. Finally, and most important, I believe that both pluralists and their critics have become sidetracked by epistemological issues and that pluralists have made the wrong sort of general argument for their position. Until this defect is remedied, the debate over social justice will remain sidetracked.

Walzer and others have tried to show, by linking their substantive views to a more basic epistemological position, that a systematic theory of justice is impossible. Hence, Walzer argues from moral relativism to a pluralistic view of justice in the following way: all propositions about social justice are matters of social convention; conceptual analysis reveals that our own sense of justice is characterized by a plurality of first principles; in our society, therefore, an appropriate theory of justice must be pluralistic.

There are two related difficulties with this sort of argument. The first is that it is quite possible to reach very similar substantive conclusions from quite different epistemological positions. As Rawls observed quite some time ago, pluralism is simply the view that "the complexity of the moral facts defies our efforts to give a full account of our judgments and necessitates a plurality of competing principles. How far such a view is committed to certain epistemological theories is a separate question."[12] Thus, David Ross, one of the most prominent pluralists of an earlier day, argued for a theory of justice in many respects similar to Walzer's from epistemological assumptions that were very different. For Ross, the fact that justice is a matter of several competing principles is guaranteed by our intuitive knowledge of a moral order that is *independent* of the conventions of any particular society.

Second, even when theorists agree at a metaethical level they may still disagree about the degree of precision we can eventually achieve from substantive first principles. For example, neither Rawls nor Walzer subscribes to the rational intuitionist view that moral objectivity is given by "a moral order prior to and independent of our conceptions of social cooperation and the person."[13] Both believe that we can achieve a "suitably objective" theory of justice by formulating "the deeper basis of agreement in our culture."[14] The only difference is that Rawls goes further in trying "to originate and fashion starting points for justification by connecting them up with a wide range of considered judgments."[15] Nevertheless, Rawls believes we can eventually justify a conception of justice that is quite systematic, while Walzer does not. As these examples illustrate, it is quite unlikely that we can demonstrate the impossibility of a systematic theory of justice on epistemological grounds alone, as Walzer tries to do. And it is just as unlikely that we can dispense with pluralism by a similar strategy, for example, by attacking Walzer as a "relativist."[16] Walzer's substantive view of justice may be correct, even if there are difficulties with his metaethics.

The fact that Rawls and contemporary pluralists use somewhat different methods of justification leads to the second difficulty with Walzer's argument. Although Rawls appears to accept the idea that principles of justice must in some sense be understood relative to the conventions or "implicit ideals" of a particular society, his method of justification is designed both to extend and revise our conventional opinions. In attempting to justify a conception of justice in "wide reflective equilibrium," Rawls tries to connect first principles of justice not only to our "considered judgments" but to various "background" theories as well, for example, a conception of the person, assumptions about social cooperation, and the general facts of social theory. In principle, no belief at any level is considered beyond revision; thus, Rawls believes he can eventually replace pluralism with a set of "priority rules." But there is nothing in the epistemological position of Walzer and other contemporary pluralists that would preclude this sort of extension, that is, no reason in principle why Rawls's argument should be regarded as anything more than an attempt to build upon views that Walzer and others already share. This means that when Walzer and others contrast their own method of justification with that of Rawls, as they often do with great flourish, they are missing the point; indeed, their failure to engage Rawls's argument at this level appears to be almost complete. Rawls's method of justification *anticipates* the epistemological views of the pluralists and is designed to take over at just the point where their views fail. Any convincing pluralist critique of Rawls must begin with this recognition.

It seems, then, that there is no necessary connection between pluralism and any particular epistemological doctrine; and even if there were, it would have little relevance to the debate between Rawls and his pluralist critics, all of whom are in basic agreement at the metaethical level. These two points bring us back to the necessity of directly assessing the substantive merits of alternative theories of social justice, for if these observations are correct, there is no other way of dealing with the question at hand. As Rawls remarks, once the issue is posed in this manner, "it is pointless to discuss [it] in the abstract. The [pluralist] and his critic will have to settle this question once the latter has put forward his more systematic account."[17] In trying to provide overwhelming epistemological arguments of the sort mentioned above, contemporary pluralists have failed to make the kind of argument they must make if they are to engage their rivals in a significant way. By beginning with a "commonsensical" view of what philosophy can accomplish, Walzer in particular appears to beg the question, for he *begins* with a view of the limits of political philosophy that he is only entitled to (if he is entitled to it at all) at the *end* of a serious examination of the alternatives.

This kind of argumentation will not do: the alternatives must be canvased in a much more fruitful way. My aim is to provide a framework for analysis that leads to more profitable comparisons by focusing on the problems created by different "units of analysis," or, to use Rawlsian terms, different conceptions of the "primary subject" of social justice. By examining such notions as "the basic structure," "spheres of justice," and the "overall situation" of each individual, I try to determine the sort of precision that can reasonably be expected from a theory of social justice. This issue is of central importance, for as Aristotle observed, "It is the mark of an educated man to look for precision in each class of things so far as the nature of the subject admits."[18]

NOTES

1. Dworkin, "What Is Equality? Part Two: Equality of Resources."
2. Dworkin, "To Each His Own," p. 5.
3. Ibid.
4. Ibid.
5. Walzer, " 'Spheres of Justice'," p. 44.
6. Rawls, *A Theory of Justice,* p. 88.
7. Ibid., p. 80.
8. Rawls, "The Basic Structure as Subject," p. 65.
9. Rawls, "The Basic Structure as Subject," p. 63.
10. Dworkin, "To Each His Own," p. 4.
11. This summary of the varieties of pluralism closely follows Rawls's discussion in *A Theory of Justice,* pp. 35-36.
12. Ibid., p. 35.
13. Rawls, "Kantian Constructivism in Moral Theory," p. 536.
14. Ibid., p. 539.
15. Ibid.
16. By virtue of their common rejection of rational intuitionism, the metaethics of Rawls and contemporary pluralists resemble each other much more than either resembles the metaethics of Henry Sidgwick or David Ross. But this is not to say that there are no metaethical disagreements at all between Rawls and many contemporary pluralists. Of course, it might be argued that if objectivity is guaranteed by a moral order prior to and independent of our moral practices, then neither the conventionalism of Walzer nor the "constructivism" of Rawls can be accepted. But, again, it does not really matter *how* we explain moral objectivity. If we accept "rational institutionism" as a general account of the objectivity of our moral judgments, we must still explain how the independent moral order we discern by intuition should be characterized. As Rawls observes, rational intuitionism is itself "compatible with a variety of contents, for example, the monistic utilitarianism of Sidgwick and the pluralistic intuitionism of Ross" ("Kantian Constructivism in Moral Theory," p. 557). Given persistent disagreement over principles that are supposedly "self-evident," providing this sort of explanation appears to be a rather large task. (For further discussion, see Daniels, "Wide Reflective Equilbrium and Theory Acceptance in Ethics.")
17. Ibid, p. 39.
18. Aristotle, *Nicomachean Ethics,* p. 936.

CHAPTER 2

The Basic Structure
and Personal Desert

In "The Basic Structure as Subject," John Rawls tries to establish the following claims:

> First, that once we think of the parties to a social contract as free and equal (and rational) moral persons, then there are strong reasons for taking the basic structure as the primary subject. Second, that in view of the distinctive features of this structure, the initial agreement, and the conditions under which it is made, must be understood in a special way that distinguishes this agreement from all others; third, doing this allows a Kantian view to take account of the profoundly social nature of human relationships. And finally, that while a large element of pure procedural justice transfers to the principles of justice, these principles must nevertheless embody an ideal form for the basic structure in the light of which ongoing institutional processes are to be constrained and the accumulated results of individual transactions continually adjusted.[1]

In this chapter I reverse the order of these considerations and first try to explain the various ways in which Rawls offers a "pure procedural" theory of justice, thereby clarifying his assertion that principles of justice must embody an "ideal form" for the basic structure. Next, I try to show why Rawls focuses on principles for institutions by considering some of the problems that emerge when we instead regard principles of personal desert as fundamental. I argue that distinctive features of the basic structure, particularly the central role played by markets, rule out principles of individual economic desert as a starting point for evaluating the overall design of social institutions. Finally, I consider why someone like Rawls must assume that the parties to a social contract are free and equal and associated in terms of a special common purpose, that of securing the conditions necessary to the effective exercise of their moral powers. By reversing Rawls's discussion in this way, I hope to show that the idea of the basic structure plays an important independent role in his theory and that the idea of the basic structure allows Rawls to approach the problem of social justice in a way that differs fundamentally from that of other recent theorists. As noted earlier, however, my purpose is not to defend Rawls's theory of justice. Rather, it is to explain the reasons and consequences of Rawls's decision to make the basic structure his primary focus of attention.

The Basic Structure and Procedural Justice

As Hugo Bedau first observed some time after the initial wave of critical response to Rawls, the question of what a theory of justice is about forms a central axis of disagreement about justice. Bedau argues that there have been two major ways of thinking about justice.[2] Traditionally, political theorists have been concerned with *distributive* justice, the principles governing the allocation of a common stock of goods to individuals. More recently, however, they have been concerned with *social* justice, the principles governing the design of the basic economic and political institutions that form the background against which individual claims arise. Bedau contends that this second conception of justice was unique when it first appeared in Rawls's work and that because the importance of this distinction has not been fully appreciated, much of the criticism directed at Rawls has been beside the point.

Although Bedau is correct about the importance of this initial distinction, I believe he overemphasizes the novelty of Rawls's views. Part of the "institutional thesis" Bedau ascribes to Rawls is simply too strong. Nevertheless, Bedau has understood Rawls's rationale for focusing on social institutions better than most other critics. For this reason, consideration of Bedau's interpretation will serve as a useful introduction to the idea of the basic structure.

We begin with Bedau's central question: What sort of thing has been or could be considered the primary subject of the predicate "justice"? Bedau considers five possibilities: persons, in virtue of their character or acts; the acts themselves; the character of persons manifested by those acts; the pattern of goods distributed among persons; and the basic social institutions that control the distribution of goods (Rawls's position).[3] According to Bedau, we can quickly eliminate persons and their dispositions as possible primary subjects of justice.[4] These are analytically derivative because one is just or has a just character only if one acts or has a propensity to act in a certain way. We must therefore compare the thesis that justice is primarily an attribute of social institutions with the remaining two views. Theorists who believe that justice resides primarily in actions or in patterns have written "as if they had an independent criterion for the justice or injustice of the distribution of goods in society." In other words, they have written "as if it does not matter much what the character of social institutions is as long as the outcome of their operation satisfies that criterion."[5] Rawls, on the other hand, is said to believe that no such criterion exists and that the question of institutional structure is in any case prior. Bedau argues that these two claims comprise Rawls's "institutional thesis" about the subject of justice.[6]

Let us consider the second part of Rawls's institutional thesis first. Why does he believe institutional justice is prior to justice between individuals? We ordinarily think of justice in terms of commonsense precepts that apply directly to individuals, for example, principles of need and desert. But Rawls argues that these precepts cannot be fundamental because they are inadequate for a theory of justice directly related to "the background system."[7] Furthermore, the effects of that system are so pervasive and complex that it is quite difficult to apply commonsense precepts to them directly. At the same time the influence of our basic institutions can hardly be ignored. Bedau writes:

> On any theory of social justice, a given action of a person either depends upon (as when, for example, it amounts to administration of) the basic social structure, or it does not. Where it does, then the structure of the institution in question is decisive because the action simply transmits or applies in a particular instance the features of the institution itself. Where it does not, if the institutional thesis is correct, the action of the individual is of no great consequence one way or the other so far as social justice is concerned, because its effects will in time be blunted or effaced by interference from basic social institutions. On any alternative, therefore, the powerful impact upon individual action from basic social institutions is inescapable. If justice is to prevail in society, then the principles of justice cannot ignore the structure of the basic social institutions.[8]

There is, then, an initially plausible reason for accepting the second part of Rawls's thesis, namely, institutions must be the primary subject of justice because of their causal importance. Rawls lists the Constitution, the recognized forms of property, and the market as examples of major institutions, all of which establish the background against which individuals act and partially determine the character of those actions.

So far, however, the institutional thesis seems vague. In what ways do institutions influence individual action? Why are those institutions Rawls lists basic and not a different set? Bedau criticizes Rawls on this score, faulting him for not providing a body of social scientific generalizations that would tell us which institutions are basic in a causal sense. His reasoning is that without such information basic institutions can only be defined as those that are necessary or sufficient to implement principles of justice, "and this leaves us still uncertain what those institutions are."[9] Bedau therefore maintains that Rawls' institutional thesis is important but only in a programmatic sense. He argues that the theory of social justice must await our ability

> to identify and measure the effects of the basic institutions upon persons and to construct the appropriate counterfactual generalizations of what personal character, aspiration, and conduct would be like in the absence of actual basic social institutions and in the presence of different set. Unless these matters can be handled relatively reliably, we will have reason to doubt whether a theory of social justice ought to be primarily about the basic institutional structure of society, or—what is worse— reason to doubt whether a theory of social justice can be developed at all or actually implemented to any great extent in human life.[10]

In other words, Rawls's thesis that the basic structure is the first subject of social justice may well be true. But, according to Bedau, we know so little about how basic institutions actually work that there is no way of really evaluating this thesis at present and certainly no way of implementing it successfully.

Insofar as Bedau emphasizes the way in which a theory of justice for the basic structure depends on reliable generalizations about how institutions may be expected to work, there is good reason to agree with him. In Chapter 6, I illustrate this dependence by considering the way in which Rawls tries to meet various objections to his theory by claiming that, as an empirical matter, certain kinds of distributive problems tend not to arise in a well-ordered society. In the present context, however, the importance of Bedau's objection is that it leads to an even deeper criticism of Rawls, for Bedau believes that Rawls's definition of the basic structure is not just vague but incoherent as well, given his emphasis on pure procedural justice. This criticism rests on a misunderstanding of Rawls's thesis that must be cleared up.

Bedau's objection that it is incoherent to define basic institutions in terms of first principles stems from the first part of Rawls's "institutional thesis." Recall that Rawls claims it is impossible to arrive at an independent criterion of distribution according to which the results produced by institutions can be assessed. As Bedau explains, "because Rawls denies any such criterion exists he is driven to a position in which the basic institutional structure, in conjunction with 'pure procedural justice' alone must suffice."[11] But if justice is a pure procedural matter, Bedau continues, then the basic structure cannot be defined as any and all institutions necessary to produce a certain pattern of distribution—for Rawls has already disavowed the possibility of describing such a pattern. Another critic, David Miller, makes the same point:

"Had Rawls wished to make his account of justice pure procedural, he should have omitted his two principles altogether and prescribed only an institutional framework. . . . But in Rawls's case the institutions are set up to *satisfy* the two principles."[12] The problem, according to Bedau, Miller, and others, is not that Rawls's definition of the basic structure is too general or vague. Rather, his failure to provide an empirical explanation of which institutions are basic is a logical one. On this view, only an empirical definition of the basic structure, in terms of its effects on persons, could be consistent with Rawls's reasons for taking institutions as the primary subject in the first place, that is, by hypothesis, no other way of defining the basic structure is available.

If we attend more closely to the text, however, we will see that this criticism is misguided. According to Rawls, "the intuitive idea is to design the social system so that the *outcome* is fair, at least *within a certain range*."[13] Here Rawls acknowledges that his theory is not, in one sense, a pure procedural one. A fair distribution is assessed according to whether it satisfies equal liberty under fair opportunity and the difference principle. These are criteria for assessing the *results* of the social process, as Rawls's critics point out. But the phrase, "within a certain range" is important, as shown by the contrast Rawls goes on to make: "If it is asked in the abstract whether one distribution of a given stock of things to definite individuals with known desires and preferences is better than another, then there is no answer to this question. The conception of the two principles does not interpret the primary problem of social justice as one of allocative justice."[14]

By contrasting pure procedural with allocative justice, Rawls is claiming that principles of social justice cannot be used to assign or reassign goods or positions to specific people. Rather, individuals must assign themselves their own positions within institutions. Institutions are deemed fair because they produce outcomes "within a certain range." In Rawls's theory, this range is defined by the expectations of "representative positions," not by any particular individual's expectations. When Rawls says that the theory of justice does not have independent criteria for a fair distribution he is easily misunderstood. What he means is that there are no criteria for fair outcomes to specific individuals. There are, however, independent criteria for assessing the overall outcome of a process that leaves the matter of individual shares largely indeterminate. Rawls's two principles are meant to provide just such criteria.

The distinctive mark of Rawls's conception of social justice is the absence of independent criteria for a fair distribution to specific individuals. But critics of Rawls are wrong when they infer that a pure procedural theory must preclude any criteria whatsoever for assessing the results that institutions produce. Indeed, Rawls is still concerned with outcomes, not institutions, but he is interested in class, not individual, outcomes. Once justice to the relevant class or classes has been established, social justice has no more to say about individual claims. The real subject of a theory of social justice, therefore, is still a pattern rather than any particular set of institutions. But the subject of a theory of social justice is a pattern of *positions*, not *individual holdings*.

Briefly, for Rawls, justice is procedural at three levels. At the levels of justification and individual shares, this theory is indeed "pure procedural." At both levels, Rawls specifies fair background conditions and then accepts whatever is chosen in those conditions as fair. At the level of institutions, however, justice is an "imperfect procedural" matter. We select just institutions and regulate their operation by trying to approximate the general results demanded by whatever principles are chosen in the original position. This is what Rawls means when he says that the principles of justice must "embody an ideal form for the basic structure." In other words, Rawls believes that the basic structure is the primary subject of the attribute *justice*: institutions, not individual holdings, are to be assessed in terms of first principles. But first principles or the kind of patterns demanded by them are the subject of a *theory* of justice. This is a weaker thesis than the one Bedau presents. Rawls's thesis is not so novel as to preclude any reference to patterns.

The Basic Structure and Personal Desert as a Possible Criterion of Social Justice

Now that we have a better sense of what it means to say that the basic structure is the first subject of justice, what makes this view plausible? As Bedau remarks, insofar as Rawls has an argument that social justice is a matter of pure procedural justice, constrained by the institutions of the basic structure, its fundamental form is that of a disjunctive syllogism: (1) there are only three kinds of justice to begin with, namely, imperfect, perfect, and pure procedural justice; (2) the first two must be ruled out because we cannot arrive at any satisfactory independent criteria for a just distribution to individuals; thus, (3) social justice must be a matter of pure procedural justice "as long as utter skepticism about the possibility of a theory of justice does not take over."[15] Obviously, if this is the structure of Rawls's argument then the second premise contains the crucial step. Why does Rawls rule out the possibility of arriving at *any* satisfactory independent principles of distribution to specific individuals? After all, virtually every principle of justice that has been proposed before and since *A Theory of Justice* has been of this sort. Each has been intended as a standard for assessing distributive shares independently of the procedures that produce them.

Unfortunately, Rawls's claim is so sweeping that a satisfactory answer to this question cannot be given all at once. We can, however, provide at least part of the answer by considering Rawls's reasons for rejecting principles of personal desert. This is the obvious place to start because principles of desert offer the clearest alternative to pure procedural justice. They provide external standards for assessing the outcomes of distributive procedures, like the market. And, unlike the principle of utility and certain other candidate principles of social justice, they have the added attraction of being both retrospective and extremely sensitive to differences between individuals. Great interest therefore attaches to the question of why Rawls rejects personal desert as a criterion of social justice. For in so doing, Rawls provides part of the rationale for his own approach.

In the following section, I first set aside Rawls's view that the bases of personal desert are themselves undeserved and therefore "arbitrary from a moral point of view." Once this radical rejection of desert is set aside, we can focus on two, more important questions. The first question is whether basic institutions can in practice be set up to accurately measure and reward personal desert. At least in the case of economic desert, I show that there are several features of the market that cast serious doubt on this possibility, although I do not think they give us grounds for dismissing the idea of economic desert completely. The second question is whether we can distinguish claims of desert from claims of "legitimate expectation." This question reveals one of the central problems that motivates both Rawls's work and most of the alternative theories of justice considered in the following chapters. Virtually all recent theorists of social justice agree that principles of economic desert cannot be regarded as fundamental because they cannot be used to specify the initial context within which desert claims first arise. This is not to say the individuals cannot acquire desert on the basis of undeserved abilities; rather, it is to point out that principles of desert cannot be used to settle the question of how and why social opportunities for desert should first be distributed. Nozick, Dworkin, Ackerman, and others try to solve this problem either by going back to a "state of nature" or by imagining a hypothetical "initial situation" in which individual holdings are first determined on some other basis. Such devices are then used to determine the context within which claims of desert, or legitimate expectation, first emerge. Rawls thinks this approach is unworkable, and argues instead that context and scope of desert must be defined in terms of the general purposes of a well-ordered society, which define the positions that the community is interested in and the procedures for filling those positions. These procedures convert all claims of desert into claims of legitmate expectation.

Of course, both approaches may ultimately fail. We may be forced to give up both the idea of organizing the basic structure in terms of a set of overarching goals and the alternative project of imagining a pristine "initial situation" in which social opportunities for desert have not yet been handed out. In this case, we will have no choice but to try to assess our historical practices of rewarding desert in a rather piecemeal fashion, without looking for some comprehensive perspective from which to judge all of the opportunities for acquiring desert that individuals might enjoy. But before reaching this conclusion, we must first try to understand recent theories of justice on their own terms, and this means concerning ourselves with the various attempts that have been made to specify an "initial situation" within which claims of desert and entitlement can arise. This is the problem of social justice as recent theorists have posed it. In discussing Rawls's reasons for rejecting personal desert, therefore, we are also framing the problem that other theorists have tried to solve in a different way.

Rawls's Radical Rejection of Desert

Rawls's reasons for completely rejecting the idea of personal desert have been often discussed. A short summary is unavoidable, however, as a prelude to setting this part of his argument aside. In section 17 of *A Theory of Justice*, Rawls argues that no one can be considered deserving on the basis of their natural talents, initial social position, or personal efforts. Rawls's argument, of course, is that all of these desert-bases are themselves undeserved: No one is responsible for individual success in the natural lottery, initial social advantages, or the encouragement and support received from family and friends. But if no one has earned the resources that enable one to be deserving, then no one deserves the benefits that flow from those resources. On this view, the initial distribution of talent and advantage is "morally arbitrary," and this arbitrariness contaminates any subsequent distribution. Principles of justice must therefore rest on some other, nonarbitrary grounds, that is, on the capacity for justice that Rawls assumes is characteristic of all members of a well-ordered society.

This argument is too well known to require further elaboration. I will be equally brief with the way in which Nozick and many others have rebutted it. First, it is not the case that we only apply the concept of desert when the basis of desert is itself deserved. Excellence is often thought to deserve recognition despite the fact that achievement "comes naturally." More important, we could not employ the concept of desert any differently. For requiring every basis of desert to be itself deserved would lead to an infinite regress. Of course, we could conclude from this that personal desert does not exist at all. But this conclusion simply begs the question and leaves unexplained how an antidesert theorist, Rawls for example, can hold that the capacity for justice, itself undeserved, makes us deserving of justice. In short, the argument proves too much.

Although these objections have seemed decisive to most commentators, there is one possible line of response that should be considered before Rawls's radical rejection of desert is put to one side. As George Sher has demonstrated, it is possible to reformulate Rawls's position in a way that avoids the question begging and regress noted above.[16] Sher begins by allowing that individuals *can* deserve on the basis of undeserved or "basic" abilities. Nevertheless, Sher points out that individuals cannot have different personal deserts when an initial distribution of basic abilities is so unequal that reasonable competitive efforts are made impossible for some people. In other words, Sher acknowledges the general criticisms of Rawls's argument above, but tries to save part of that argument by confining it to competitive contexts. In competitive contexts, individuals can deserve to win on the basis of undeserved abilities, but only if their initial assets do not make the very idea of competition a mockery. Since it seems plausible that the central problem of social justice involves the fairness of profits and wages in a competitive context, the market, Sher's reformulated version of Rawls's argument seems promising. Sher argues, however, that this reformulated version also fails.

Sher points out that individuals can usually compensate for a deficiency in one basic ability through the exercise of another, that is, Jones is smarter, but Smith tries harder. Individuals can also choose *where* to make efforts, which means that generally they are capable of making whatever efforts are necessary to achieve *equal well-being,* even if they are not capable of making reasonable competitive efforts in every specific context.[17] Sher argues that these conditions seem sufficient to protect the notion of economic desert, since the capacity to make reasonable competitive efforts at every task seems too demanding as a condition of fair economic competition overall.

Finally, where individuals are unequally deserving, this can be explained not only by different compensating efforts and choices of occupation, but also by differing individual attentiveness to well-being in the first place.[18] In short, Sher argues that there is little reason to think that different basic abilities offer the best explanation of inequality, therefore little reason to adopt a principle for redressing the general distribution of those abilities. Note, however, that Sher does not question the reformulated antidesert argument itself, so much as its application. He accepts that individuals cannot deserve to win when effective competition is precluded, but tries to show that such competiton is rarely precluded by the distribution of basic abilities alone. For this reason, the "different abilities" argument fails, even when reformulated. Unless another line of argument is open, personal desert must qualify as a fundamental principle of social justice.

This brief review indicates why any further attempt at refurbishing Rawls's radical rejection of desert must almost certainly prove fruitless. The general considerations against such a project, together with Sher's more detailed argument, simply tell too strongly. Nevertheless, the results of this review have not been entirely negative. It is at least clear that any defense of Rawls's overall position requires a new point of departure. And Sher's own argument suggests the direction we should take.

Practical Grounds for Dismissing Claims of Economic Desert

The Role of Luck and Competence in the Market
Until recently, philosophical discussions of Rawls's position have usually concerned the question of whether individuals can ever be said to be deserving. But Sher suggests that we simply acknowledge this possibility and instead inquire about the necessary contexts for different kinds of desert. In the case of economic desert, this suggests a reversal of our usual order of inquiry. Rather than asking whether individuals are *in principle* capable of deserving, it seems more profitable to ask instead whether institutions for the basic structure, particularly markets, are *in practice* capable of giving individuals what they deserve.

Consider the role of "luck" in modern market systems. If we consult empirical studies of income distribution, it appears that luck or chance is surprisingly important. Economists as different as Hayek and Lester Thurow, for example, stress that in market systems the relation between individual income and such "deterministic" variables as education, skills, and age is slight. In fact, empirical studies note that only 20 to 30 percent of individual income variance can be explained by these variables, which means that unknown or stochastic factors play a very large role in the market.[19] Consequently, it is difficult to explain variance in *individual* (not group) holdings as the result of background discrimination or uneven abilities. If we turn from the economists to the sociologists, we only find this picture confirmed. To take just one well-known example, the Jencks study of inequality discovered only 12 to 15 percent less inequality among men of similar family background, cognitive skills, educational attainment, and occupational status than among individuals randomly selected for comparison. That study concluded, or rather speculated, that individual income variance may therefore depend primarily on "competence" and "luck," two "residual" categories that reflect the low correlation of other variables formerly thought to be important.[20]

Studies such as those performed by Jencks and others are apt to change our view of the market, even though the details and more specific conclusions of such studies remain controversial. Such studies indicate that, with respect to individual income, a modern market economy may more nearly resemble a lottery than a competition. The lesson that has been drawn by many political theorists, particularly egalitarians, is that income and occupation depend on luck or chance more than anything else.

Of course, egalitarian theorists have long emphasized the role of luck in explaining why market arrangements are unfair. For several reasons, however, it seems mistaken to make luck or chance a decisive consideration against the market. To begin with, the findings of studies by Jencks and others obviously cut both ways. On the one hand, even conservative critics like Daniel Bell have had to concede that, "there is much more luck to the occupational system than Marxists or Meritocrats would like to believe." On the other hand, as Bell goes on to note, " 'common observation' (that other residual category of analysis) would indicate that—again, on the professional level at least—hard work is a necessary condition of success."[21] In other words, in the absence of any determinate measure, it remains an open question which "residual" factor, "luck" or "competence," is the most important source of inequality. We simply cannot estimate the relative importance of luck and competence precisely.

In any case, the fact that chance plays a role in the allocation of individual holdings is by itself hardly an argument that actual market systems are not meritocratic enough to deserve the name. For unless we adopt the position that social justice requires the elimination of *all* contingency from human affairs, a certain amount of luck or chance must be considered permissible in any just economic system. Indeed, all that seems to be required is a fairly rough correlation between ideal and actual patterns of reward.[22] Without being able to measure something as vague and encompassing as "competence," however, the extent to which market systems approximate ideal meritocratic patterns must remain an open question.

Then again, distributive outcomes attributed to luck may sometimes be better understood as the results of general macroeconomic policies. As such, they are partially subject to our control. In other words, even if chance now appears to play too large a role in the market, it may be possible to improve this situation somewhat through institutions designed to register desert more precisely. By emphasizing the role of luck, it is certainly possible to cast doubt on the meritocratic character of actual markets. But, for the above reasons, stressing the role of luck does not seem sufficient to discredit the notion of competitive economic desert. Luck is not, however, the only feature of modern economic systems that must be taken into account.

The Role of Desert in Allocating Tasks

Thus far, I have been discussing the possibility of markets awarding income and tasks on the basis of competitve desert: those who win competitive contests according to the rules become deserving by definition. There is another sense of desert, however, that depends on the idea of a relationship of appropriateness or "fit" between a person, act, or quality and a particular thing. It is in virtue of this relationship of appropriateness, rather than by virtue of the rules of a contest, that desert is acquired. It is especially important to distinguish these two models of desert-acquisiton. For it has been suggested that markets might recognize either kind of desert. If markets do work with the idea of desert as "appropriate fit," they might very well fail to satisfy conditions of fair competition between all members of the economy, yet still reward the deserving from among that small pool of candidates that is considered for any particular job. This is in fact Sher's suggestion. According to Sher, "there may be good reason to reject the competitive model of desert-acquisition even here. Put simply, the suggestion is that the best qualified claimant's desert may arise, not through any victory over his rivals, but directly from the comparative closeness of the 'fit' between his qualifications and the requirements of the job or opportunity to be awarded."[23] In other words, the way in which the market rewards desert may have less to do with "winning" than with finding a particularly appropriate "match" between superior abilities and specific tasks. Of course, this suggestion complicates matters. But it does so in a helpful way, by forcing us to take a closer look at the way in which markets actually function. Although Sher's alternative way of understanding desert-acquisition has much to recommend it, particularly in noneconomic contexts, I believe we must reject it as an explanation of economic desert. We must do so because markets work with a very limited definition of what makes persons deserving. Technically speaking, markets register "merit," not "desert."

As Norman Daniels has pointed out, there is ordinarily some confusion about the reasons we have for awarding tasks to those of superior ability.[24] Normally, we think of meritocratic job placement as a "microprinciple," directing us to select the best available individual for each particular job. And we think of meritocratic job placement in this way because we understand the principle to be one of individual justice. Those with superior abilities *deserve* certain tasks. Our conventional understanding, then, seems to be in keeping with Sher's suggestion about how we acquire desert: we do so by virtue of an appropriate fit between our abilities and particular tasks.

It is always possible, however, to examine our conventional understanding of desert, in order to see exactly what conception of appropriateness or "fit" is presupposed. More important, it is always possible to ask about the point of a conventional practice, in order to see whether our ordinary understanding of it agrees with its underlying rationale. What, then, is the basic rationale for singling out some abilities as more meritorious in the first place? Clearly, in the context of hiring for a particular job, the answer must be that having certain abilities leads to greater productivity. But if the underlying rationale in this case is productivity, then, as Daniels remarks, "there is something anomalous about basing a merit claim . . . on claims about micro-productivity while at the same time ignoring macro-productivity considerations."[25] In other words, there is no reason in principle for thinking that considerations of *overall* productivity or efficiency should not override the more limited claims of desert that arise in micro-situations.

This conclusion yields a rather surprising result. On this view, a person may "merit" a particular job without thereby "deserving" it. A particular person may very well "fit" a job, in virtue of his superior abilities, and thus in one sense "deserve" that job more than anyone else; but provided there is someone else who can do the same job well enough, considerations of overall efficiency may nevertheless dictate that the person of superior ability be placed elsewhere. In principle, the economic desert, or "merit," of an individual is determined by assignment to a job within the most productive array of job assignments overall, *not* by determining whether they are the best person for a particular job, per se.[26] In order to be perfectly consistent with the underlying rationale of meritocratic job placement, a meritocracy must employ meritocratic job placement as a "macro" principle for the basic structure as a whole.

In trying to use meritocratic job placement in this way, however, we inevitably run into difficulties. Obviously, no central agency can directly select the single maximally productive job array (or set of job arrays) from all those possible and then assign tasks on the basis of predictions about how matching particular individuals to particular tasks will increase overall productivity (although we will see an attempt to imagine such a situation in Chapter 5, where Galston's theory is discussed).[27] We cannot even begin to approximate such macroemployment in practice. Modern economic systems must instead rely on markets to assign and commensurate the indefinite number of tasks that such systems require. Given the necessity of relying on markets, however, there can be at best only a very rough correlation between overall productivity and the assignment of appropriate tasks. The only way that tasks can be assigned according to merit is by guaranteeing background conditions which establish fair equality of opportunity. Note, however, that in this weak sense even Rawls's theory can be said to be meritocratic with respect to job placement.[28] Let me emphasize again, however, that this is so only in a weak sense. In Rawls's "well-ordered society" a particular individual ends up with a job if he is the best person for *that* job. No effort is made to calculate whether hiring a particular person best contributes to *overall* productivity, and in fact we completely lack the information necessary for such calculations.

What Daniels has uncovered is a discrepancy between the way in which markets actually work and their underlying rationale. In principle, markets are merely an imperfect mechanism for efficient job placement: no qualification of individual "fitness" or desert for a particular job overrides the requirements of the productive system as a whole. But, in practice, markets do tend to reward the deserving, rather than the meritorious, in at least one sense. For as decentralized institutions, markets do not aim at a "maximally productive job array." Instead, each employer in the market selects from a restricted pool the person who best "fits" his needs, without the benefit of a survey of the entire labor supply or structure of the economy.

This discrepancy between the underlying rationale for meritocratic job placement and the results of the market explains why we ordinarily tend to waver between regarding job placement as a matter of efficiency and as a matter of individual justice. It also explains why both Daniels's model of desert acquisition, which emphasizes "macro" considerations, and Sher's model, which emphasizes "micro" considerations, both seem to partially fit the facts. The way in which we regard the possibility of personal economic desert depends on the perspective adopted. From the macroproductivity point of view, we must conclude that in principle individuals can only deserve their jobs in the way explained by Daniels. And this of course matches Rawls's perspective, which approaches the question of social justice in terms of the basic structure. It may turn out, however, that we cannot find a single perspective from which to coordinate the basic structure as a whole. In this case, considerations of microproductivity, or individual "fit," may have to be regarded, by default, as the relevant basis for assigning tasks.[29] This is roughly the view presented by Michael Walzer and other "commonsense" pluralists, who reject the idea of coordinating different spheres of distribution in terms of a single, overall goal, like the advantage of the least well-off. Assuming for the moment, however, that we are taking the basic structure as the primary subject of justice, it would appear that individuals cannot deserve their jobs in the way Sher suggests. The actual operation of markets appears to suggest otherwise, but their underlying rationale is one of efficiency, not desert.

The Role of Desert in Allocating Income

Turning now from the problem of allocating tasks to that of allocating income, a very similar set of difficulties present themselves. As Daniels points out, there is of course no necessary connection between the principles that are appropriate to each particular case: a principle of meritocratic job placement can be combined with any number of principles for the distribution of income.[30] We might, for example, emphasize merit with respect to job placement and equality with respect to wages. But let us assume that in allocating income we also wish to adopt a principle of distribution in proportion to contribution. Markets are again the only practicable mechanism for implementing such a principle, and markets again narrowly limit the possibilities for acquiring desert.

Proponents of the idea of "comparable worth" may find the first part of this assertion objectionable. To forestall argument, then, let us also assume that in some instances we may be able to compare directly the contributions of individuals performing roughly similar jobs and tasks. Even so, there does not appear to be any standard measure for directly determining the relative value of all of the diverse sorts of tasks performed across the economy as a whole. Instead, we must rely on markets to indicate, through wages, the relative worth of various economic activities. How else, for example, are the relative contributions of those who perform such different tasks as nurse and jockey to be compared and graded, except by reference to market demand?

The point has been made often, and I need not belabor it. In relying on markets to measure individual contribution we once again slip from the idea of desert to that of merit. Markets simply ignore most of the features that we ordinarily believe relevant to the notion of personal desert. We ordinarily believe that individuals who make special efforts or sacrifices should be compensated proportionately. But conscientious effort and sacrifice frequently fail to produce anything valuable. And where there is a gap between effort and accomplishment, the market recognizes only the latter. While markets may measure our usefulness to others, as determined by a demand for our abilities, they do not measure our efforts and sacrifices except as these *happen* to benefit others. As Nozick remarks, "life is not a race in which all compete for a prize which someone has established; there is no unified race with some person judging swiftness [or we might now add, sacrifice and effort]. . . . No centralized process judges people's use of the opportunities they had; that is not what the processes of social cooperation and exchange are for."[31]

Important as all these qualifications are, however, we must be careful not to overestimate their significance. It is true that markets leave a fair amount to chance. Markets cannot register effort and sacrifice directly, and sometimes do not register them at all. It is also true that markets probably approximate the ideal of meritocratic job placement in only a very rough way (we cannot really know, since it seems impossible to assess the relative roles of luck and competence). Nevertheless, there is normally a large "strand" of distribution according to "perceived benefit" in market societies, as Nozick, and particularly Hayek, have stressed. And there is also a limited respect in which individuals acquire their jobs through "appropriate fit" rather than by means of strict competition. These qualifications may be enough to furnish a modest defense of the meritocratic character of markets. Indeed, careful apologists have never claimed that markets reward personal desert in anything but in this very limited way. Thus, while we have qualified the idea that markets are capable of giving individuals what they deserve, we still cannot dismiss the idea completely. In any case, most recent theorists of social justice make a more fundamental criticism of the idea of personal desert that we must consider, now that we have cleared the ground of several familiar objections.

The Problem of Specifying an Initial Context for Desert

To establish the personal desert of any particular individual, we must first be able to measure their contributions. As we have seen, it may be possible to do this, very roughly, through markets. Markets, however, presuppose an initial distribution of assets and preferences, as well as a certain level of technology and a particular organization of production.

An initial distribution of assets is required because it is only through individual decisions to bid for certain skills that the value of those skills is established: individuals must have initial resources with which to bid for goods and services. An initial distribution of preferences must also be assumed because aggregate demand expresses a general desire for goods, as well as purchasing power. Finally, an initial productive system must be assumed: obviously, the technical ability of a society to produce goods will affect the patterns of demand registered by the market. The general problem facing desert theorists is that they must settle all of these matters *before* determining the desert of particular individuals. The notion of desert is therefore of no help in setting up the system that enables the theorist to determine what individuals deserve.

As we have seen, personal contribution is always measured, indirectly, in terms of aggregate supply and demand. Of course, this is actually something of an exaggeration: the value of "public goods" cannot be measured accurately by markets; the costs of "economic externalities" may also go partly unregistered; and, once again in order to forgo needless argument, we might occasionally circumvent the market altogether through measures of "comparable worth." None of these qualifications affect the main point, however. The overwhelming majority of goods and services produced by modern economies can be neither accurately commensurated nor efficiently allocated without relying on markets, that is, without relying on aggregate supply and demand. Aggregate demand, however, already presupposes some initial distribution of assets. Can we use the idea of personal desert to determine this distribution? Presumably we intend to use personal desert as a fundamental principle of justice. That is, we are seeking some independent measure of the worth of various activities as a guide to an initial distribution of resources. Unfortunately, we cannot rely on aggregate demand for this purpose unless we *already have* an initial distribution. The only way this problem can be circumvented is by assuming that, "the operation of the system over time washes out any significant effects from the initial set of holdings," a rather unlikely assumption.[32] As Nozick notes, without this assumption, reliance on personal desert is circular.

To avoid misunderstanding, consider a response that naturally arises at this point. Doesn't the argument above simply revive an objection to the idea of personal desert that has already been dealt with by critics such as Nozick and Sher? As we have already noted, Nozick argues that we cannot be required to deserve our initial assets at all. And Sher argues that undeserved or "basic" abilities do not generally preclude fair economic competition. Why, then, do we require a "starting point" for personal desert?

Sher's argument concerned the supposed obstacles presented by unequal *talents*, not unequal *initial resources*. And in fact desert theorists such as Sher generally defend the notion of equal opportunity, a notion that assumes the need to offset the disadvantages of unequal social position, if not unequal basic abilities. To be sure, individuals can sometimes overcome an intial disadvantage in social position by the same means that Sher mentions in connection with disadvantages in basic abilities, that is, by compensating efforts, choice of different occupations, and differing attentiveness to well-being in the first place. Nevertheless, unequal social position is almost universally regarded both as a more serious obstacle to acquiring desert on the basis of our undeserved natural abilities and as something that a liberal society should try to overcome. Nozick, of course, is one of the few exceptions, since he also appears to reject even the traditional liberal goal of "careers open to talents." But then, Nozick is not a desert theorist at all. Like Rawls, he dispenses with the notion of desert completely, instead basing his theory on the idea of "historical" entitlements.

I return to Nozick's position in the final section of this chapter. At this point it is sufficient to note that his defense of the general *possibility* of desert does not settle the more particular question of *which* resources individuals deserve. As Michael Sandel observes, Nozick never explains why it is that we might deserve some things, like the benefits that flow from natural talent, and not others, like the benefits that flow from initial social position.[33] Nozick avoids this question altogether because he sees that the question of initial resources is not one that desert itself can determine without circularity. The basic problem is that, without aggregate demand, that is, without an initial distribution of resources, we have no way of determining the relative value of various economic activities and therefore no means of determining personal desert. But if we cannot measure personal contribution, if, indeed, the notion of personal desert becomes unintelligible under these circumstances, then obviously principles of desert offer no solution to our problem. To solve this problem we need principles of justice that are more fundamental. Such principles would be more fundamental in the sense that they determine the conditions under which individuals become, and remain, capable of deserving.

The same observations that have been made about the necessity of assuming an initial distribution of assets can be made about the necessity for an initial distribution of preferences as well. Rather than repeat the argument above, however, it is more important to notice a number of separate, but related problems that arise from relying on market demand, that is, on preference. According to theorists such as Galston, accepting individual preferences as the primary measure of the value of resources is objectionable because there is no guarantee that people will want what is actually good for them, that is, what is truly urgent and important according to some more objective criteria. "Subjective" or preference-based definitions of value raise all of the problems long familiar from critical discussions of utilitarianism, for example, the apparent unfairness of allocating resources on the basis of "expensive tastes," the problem of "voracious needs," and the possibility of "anti-social" desires. From this perspective, it is additionally difficult to see how markets can reward the truly deserving. For we would first have to specify an initial, "correct" set of preferences for each member of society, and then somehow insure that those preferences were not distorted over time. Without such measures, the market will fail to register "real" contribution or "true" desert.

Finally, how should a desert theorist handle the problem of an initial productive system? Once markets are in play, the way in which production is organized will certainly change in response to conditions of supply and demand. But at the outset we must decide, in Galston's words, "the number of individuals sharing in a task, the division of labor within tasks, and the number and kind of tasks themselves," all without benefit of the market.[34] Obviously, the way in which a productive system is set up may deeply affect opportunites for desert acquisition. Yet these organizational questions are not something that principles of desert can themselves help us to decide (assuming for the moment that it makes any sense to "decide" about something as complicated as a productive system). There is no more reason here than in the case of initial assets to assume that the influence of these decisions will somehow disappear over time.

Taking these points together, we can now see clearly the foundations of the position attributed to Rawls at the beginning of this section. Claims of desert based on economic contribution are always made in and through a particular institutional setting that converts them into claims of "legitimate expectations." Or as Rawls puts it, "In a well-ordered society individuals acquire claims to a share of the social product by doing certain things encouraged by the existing arrangements. The legitimate expectations that arise are the other side, so to speak, to justice as fairness, and the natural duty of justice."[35] Of course, these expectations reflect commonsense precepts of justice, for example, to each according to one's effort, to each according to one's skill, due compensation for undue risk, and so on. But the way in which these precepts are assessed and weighted must be a function of the whole system of an economy: thus desert in any direct sense cannot be estimated for any particular individual in a way that would establish any definite, independent claim.

Criticisms of Rawls's view that the bases of personal desert are "morally arbitrary" are well taken as far as they go, but at least in the case of economic desert they do not meet the larger thrust of his position. It is true that undeserved capacities may serve as desert bases. But, in the case of economic reward and task allocation, this is so only from the standpoint of other individuals and private associations. In contrast, "a well-ordered society has the aim of giving justice to all its citizens, but this is not an aim that ranks their expected contributions and on that basis determines their social role. The notion of an individual's contribution to society viewed as an association . . . has no place in a Kantian view."[36] This does not mean, however, that desert ceases to be a necessary moral notion. We must continue to use the idea of desert, but in "micro" contexts where there is enough information and agreement to give the notion of desert some determinate meaning. Desert as we commonly understand it is not eliminated by making it relative to legitimate expectations. Training, skill, and effort must be used as the bases of economic allocation within modern economic systems. Nevertheless, individuals only deserve economic rewards within associations that are themselves within a larger social structure. And it seems that structure must be considered just on different grounds.

The Basic Aim of Justice as Fairness

Thus far, I have argued that Rawls can reject personal desert as a fundamental principle of economic justice without relying on the argument that natural talents and conscientious efforts are "arbitrary from a moral point of view." Instead, he can focus on the problem of accurately measuring individual contributions and the difficulty of distinguishing claims of desert from legitimate expectations. These problems are unavoidable in market economies and support Rawls's view that we cannot use principles of desert in assessing the justice of the basic structure itself. Nevertheless, many questions about the role of personal desert remain. For example, individuals would still seem to be capable of deserving from society as a whole for their political contributions. Personal desert also appears to be the only appropriate basis for awarding public honors and recognition. At a deeper level, many critics have asked whether Rawls's conception of the person is defensible. How can Rawls reject *all* forms of personal desert without stripping the self of all of its contingent attributes? As Nozick, Williams, and Sandel have stressed, justice as fairness seems to treat not only the talents and attributes but also the character, convictions, and deepest loyalties of individuals as inessential or accidental elements of personality.

Since my aim is not to defend Rawls, but to use his understanding of the problem of social justice as a foil for the assessment of other theories, there is no embarrassment involved in acknowledging the first set of criticisms. As noted at the outset, Rawls cannot completely reject the idea of personal desert in any case without undermining his own position. And in the case of political desert, there are clearly certain abilities and skills that should serve as grounds for political recognition in any society. Good practical judgment and the willingness to seek advice, for example, would seem to be political virtues whatever our larger social and political goals might be.[37] Nor can we follow the strategy of my earlier discussion, by first admitting the possibility of desert in principle and then attacking the practical procedures that are available for identifying the deserving. It is plausible to approach the notion of economic desert in this way, since the market does seem to provide an example of pure procedural justice. But the way in which we recognize and reward political desert is another matter. It is quite possible to design methods for selecting office holders according to some independent standard of fitness. And while such methods of selection are certainly instances of "imperfect" procedural justice, we have no trouble in distinguishing between the rewards that politicians "legitmately expect" and the rewards they "deserve." Indeed, we are usually all too clear about the latter.

Rawls's response to the deeper objections mentioned above is contained in a recent essay, where he distinguishes between "public" and "private" conceptions of the person. In their private affairs, citizens of a well-ordered society "may regard it as impossible to view themselves apart from certain religious, philosophical and moral convictions, or from certain attachments and loyalties."[38] These convictions and attachments may suddenly change, however, as stories of religious conversion attest. And when "private identity" does undergo a radical change, we generally recognize that there is no change in "public identity" as defined by basic law. Public identity is explained in justice as fairness by characterizing persons in terms of "two moral powers," a capacity for justice and a capacity for a conception of the good. Rawls denies that this "political" conception of the person presupposes any particular metaphysical, epistemological, or psychological doctrines about

the self: in describing persons having the two moral powers as free
and equal, justice as fairness merely expresses "a basic intuitive idea
assumed to be implicit in the public culture of a democratic society."[39]
According to Rawls, "If we look at the presentation of justice as
fairness . . . no particular metaphysical doctrine about the nature of
persons, distinctive and opposed to other metaphyscial doctrines, appears among its premises or seems required by its argument."[40] If this
"method of avoidance" is successful, then the objections raised by
Rawls's critics are beside the point. For Rawls's conception of the person
in no way denies the importance of the attachments and loyalties that
his critics are worried about.

Obviously, this response raises problems that go far beyond the scope
of this book, and for that reason I will leave any detailed consideration
of these issues aside. My purpose is to assess standards of precision
for principles of justice, not to determine whether political philosophy
can be pursued apart from metaphysics. There is, however, one aspect
of Rawls's recent emphasis on the idea of moral or "political" personality that is directly relevant to the task at hand. To explain how Rawls's
approach to the problem of social justice differs from that of other
theorists, we must understand why Rawls assumes that individuals are
free and equal and associated in terms of a special common purpose.
The main reason for making these assumptions is that it is not enough
to offer grounds for rejecting or subordinating some forms of personal
desert. Rawls's theory also requires a positive account of what the
purposes of political community should be and why that community
has first claim on certain resources. As Sandel remarks, "To show that
individuals . . . do not deserve or possess 'their' assets is not necessarily
to show that society as a whole *does* deserve or possess them."[41] The
"highest order" common purpose that Rawls assumes is characteristic
of citizens in a well-ordered society provides at least the elements of
a response to this criticism. For presumably it is through the organization
of the basic structure that we most effectively deploy resources in a
way that secures the conditions necessary for the exercise of our two
moral powers. That is the essential aim of justice as fairness.

Whether Rawls can work out his later revisions to justice as fairness
in a way that meets the objections of his critics remains to be seen. It
is clear, however, that this understanding of the purpose of a well-
ordered society explains why and how Rawls's approach differs from
that of the theorists considered in the next three chapters. It is often
thought that Rawls's theory is concerned with redressing the effects
of natural and social contingencies per se. But Rawls's later writings
show why this interpretation is mistaken. The essential aim of justice

as fairness is to secure the conditions necessary to the exercise of our two moral powers. If that aim can be achieved by allowing some natural and social inequalities, then justice as fairness does not require that such inequalities be eliminated. This distinguishes Rawls's work in a fundamental way from other theories that focus exclusively on the idea of redress. As Sandel remarks, "By regarding the distribution of talents and attributes as a common asset rather than as individual possessions, Rawls obviates the need to 'even out' endowments in order to remedy the arbitrariness of social and natural contingencies. When men 'agree to share one another's fate,' it matters less that their fates, individually, may vary."[42] This understanding of the purpose of social justice also explains Rawls's response to the central problem raised earlier, namely, the apparent impossibility of using personal desert to specify an "initial" distribution of assets, preferences, and means of production. One response to this problem has been to try to solve it by other means.

Nozick, for example, rejects the idea of personal desert as a way of settling the problem of initial assets, but thinks that the problem of initial assets is still important. He suggests that we find a starting point by going back to the acquisition of property in a "state of nature." From this baseline, we try to imagine the way in which individual holdings might have developed over time had all subsequent transactions been perfectly just. We then use this notionally perfect set of holdings as a benchmark for rectifying the real history of force and fraud. Dworkin suggests instead that we imagine a hypothetical starting point. First, we imagine an auction of all available resources, with each person having equal purchasing power. After this initial auction, holdings develop in a world inhabited by persons with perfectly equal talents. Through a series of devices which I explore in the next chapter, Dworkin then tries to show how we can adjust our own circumstances to approximate what would have occurred in this imaginary world. Similar counterfactual thought experiments are offered by Ackerman and Galston.

Rawls, however, believes that "no sense can be made of the notion of that part of an individual's social benefits that exceed what would have been their situation in another society or a state of nature."[43] And since the basic aim of justice as fairness is *not* to determine a baseline from which to redress all natural and social contingencies, Rawls is under no obligation to make sense of this notion. As Rawls stresses: "it is clear that nothing depends upon being able to identify the initial arrangement (or equality); indeed, how well-off men are in this situation plays no essential role in applying the difference principle . . . estimated gains from the situation of hypothetical equality are irrelevant, if not largely impossible to ascertain anyway."[44] The last phrase brings us back to our earlier discussion of the idea of pure procedural justice. For as Rawls explains, the strategy of leaving individual shares largely to pure procedural justice has a primarily practical rationale:

> Now the great practical advantage of pure procedural justice is that it is no longer necessary to keep track of the endless variety of circumstances and changing relative positions of particular persons. One avoids the problem of defining principles to cope with the enormous complexities which would arise if such details were relevant. . . . It is the arrangement of the basic structure that is to be judged and judged from a general point of view. . . . Unless the viewpoint of the relevant (social) positions has priority, one still has a chaos of conflicting claims.[45]

In contrast, consider Dworkin's explanation of his project:

> Equality of resources, as described here, does not single out any group [as the least-advantaged]. It aims to provide a description of (or rather a set of devices aiming at) equality of resources person by person. . . . Rawls, on the other hand, assumes that the difference principle ties justice to a class, not as a matter of second-best accommodation to some deeper version of equality, which is in principle more individualized, but because the choice in the original position, which defines even at bottom what justice is, would for practical reasons be framed in class terms from the start.[46]

The issue that I address in the next three chapters is well framed by these quotations: Rawls asserts that focusing directly on individual claims of redress is both unnecessary in principle, given the essential aim of justice as fairness, and likely to produce results that are unworkably complex, indeed, senseless. Dworkin and others respond by trying to show that in fact such an approach can be developed successfully.

In the quotation that opened this chapter, Rawls claims "that once we think of the parties to the social contract as free and equal moral persons, then there are strong reasons for taking the basic structure as subject."[47] In the course of this chapter, I have suggested that we have strong reasons for focusing on the basic structure aside from Rawls's conception of moral personality. As Bedau points out, the idea of trying to directly redress the effects of natural and social contingencies opens up the prospect of insuperable difficulties. On the face of it, there seems to be no method of accurately distinguishing the "natural," "social," and "personal" factors that explain the ways in which individuals have used their opportunities. Nor does it seem possible to establish a "baseline" for measuring departures from a situation of initial equality or a state of nature. These problems can be avoided by leaving the question of individual shares to pure procedural justice and instead seeking "an ideal form" for institutions. Nor in the economic realm does it seem possible to devise "individualized" principles of justice by falling back on the idea of personal desert. Modern economic institutions make it impossible to assess individual contributions directly. Instead, they mediate the connection between contribution and reward in a way that converts all claims of desert into claims of legitimate expectation. Finally, in the economic sphere at least, we face the theoretical problem of specifying an initial distribution of assets, preferences, and means of production. This problem arises because although individuals may in principle be capable of deserving on the basis on undeserved opportunities, we seem to require a positive account of how those opportunities should initially be distributed.

Finally, in addition to these negative reasons for focusing on the basic structure, Rawls's view of the purpose of social justice permits him to leave the question of individual redress aside. If we can secure the conditions necessary for the effective exercise of our two moral powers, there is no obligation to go further by trying to make every member of society perfectly equal. When these considerations are taken together, I believe they show that Rawls has good reason for shifting our attention from individual shares to the design of background institutions. Whether we can actually develop a theory of justice that coordinates all of our basic institutions from a single viewpoint I leave until Chapter 6. Before we can consider that question, the alternative solutions that other theorists have offered to the problems outlined in this chapter must be examined.

NOTES

1. Rawls, "The Basic Structure as Subject," p. 48.
2. Bedau, "Social Justice and Social Institutions."
3. Ibid., p. 168.
4. Ibid., p. 165.
5. Ibid.
6. Ibid., p. 172.
7. Ibid., p. 171.
8. Ibid., p. 169.
9. Ibid., p. 173.
10. Ibid., p 167.
11. Ibid., p. 175.
12. Miller, *Social Justice*, p. 45.

13. Rawls, *A Theory of Justice*, p. 87.
14. Ibid., p. 88.
15. Bedau, "Social Justice and Social Institutions," p. 172.
16. Sher, "Effort, Ability, and Personal Desert," 361-76.
17. Ibid., p. 368.
18. Ibid.
19. Friedman, "Choice, Chance and the Personal Distribution of Income," 277-79; Hayek, *The Mirage of Social Justice*, pp. 80-96; Miner, *Schooling Experience and Earnings;* Thurow, "Toward a Definition of Economic Justice," pp. 56-81.
20. Jencks et al., *Inequality: A Reassessment of the Family and Schooling in America*, pp. 226-47.
21. Bell, "On Meritocracy and Equality," p. 47, fn 7.
22. Although, once again, this is not Rawls's aim in relying on the market as a mechanism for pure procedural justice to individuals.
23. Sher, "Effort, Ability, and Personal Desert," p. 370.
24. Daniels, "Meritocracy," pp. 164-78.
25. Ibid., p. 167.
26. Ibid., p. 165.
27. Ibid., p. 168.
28. Ibid., p. 174.
29. Ibid., p. 168.
30. Ibid., p. 171.
31. Nozick, *Anarchy, State and Utopia*, p. 236.
32. Ibid., p. 158.
33. Sandel, *Liberalism and the Limits of Justice*, p. 100.
34. Galston, *Justice and the Human Good*, p. 209.
35. Rawls, *A Theory of Justice*, p. 313.
36. Rawls, "The Basic Structure as Subject," p. 60.
37. See Galston's discussion, *Justice and the Human Good*, p. 271-73.
38. Rawls, "Justice as Fairness: Political Not Metaphysical," p. 241.
39. Ibid., p. 234.
40. Ibid., p. 240.
41. Sandel, p. 100.
42. Ibid., p. 70-71.
43. Rawls, "The Basic Structure as Subject," p. 63.
44. Ibid., p. 67.
45. Rawls, *A Theory of Justice*, p. 87.
46. Dworkin, "What Is Equality: Part Two: Equality of Resources," p. 340.
47. Rawls, "The Basic Structure as Subject," p. 48.

CHAPTER 3

Dworkin on Equality of Resources

In a two-part essay, entitled "What Is Equality?" Ronald Dworkin assumes that some form of overall substantive equality between individuals is a basic requirement of social justice. In Part 1 of that essay, he argues that we cannot explain the appeal of equality as a social and political ideal unless we interpret it as requiring "equality in resources" rather than "equality in welfare." In Part 2, Dworkin tries to develop both a theoretical description of equality in resources and a set of practical devices aiming at equality under actual conditions. I will only be concerned here with Dworkin's metric for equality in resources developed in the second part of his essay. Consideration of Dworkin on equality in welfare would lead us too far afield.[1]

Dworkin's essay is by far the most sophisticated attempt to date at devising an inclusive formula for establishing individual claims on the social product. The burden of this chapter is that Dworkin's efforts only illustrate the apparent impossibility of such an undertaking. I will argue that Dworkin's theoretical description of equality in resources is deeply incoherent; and, of course, this means that Dworkin's practical suggestions for approximating that ideal also lack cogency. Even if Dworkin's theoretical ideal were sound, however, there is still a separate set of difficulties that would prevent any accurate approximation of Dworkin's ideal under actual circumstances. In short, Dworkin's metric of equality is unacceptable, even if we assume that some form of substantive equality is indeed a fundamental principle of social justice.[2]

In turning to Dworkin's theory, I now begin my assessment of recent theories of justice that focus on the overall claims of particular individuals. As explained in the last chapter, these theories attempt to take into account the effects of natural and social contingencies when evaluating the situations of each particular member of society. They also attempt to specify an initial situation in which assets are first distributed on grounds other than personal desert. Dworkin, for example, argues that ideally we should compensate individuals in strict proportion to their efforts and sacrifices (but not their talents) over a lifetime. In principle, this requires us to estimate counterfactually how individual holdings might have developed in a world where everyone has initially equal assets and abilities. As we shall see in the next chapter, Bruce Ackerman has a similar aim, although his theory does not require us to track individual claims to compensation over time in the same way. Ackerman proposes what is in effect an extremely inclusive notion of equal opportunity, one that involves commensurating all of the initial disadvantages that individuals can possibly suffer. Resources are then redistributed so that the sum of initial disadvantages that each individual must suffer are made equal.

Even at the very outset, such theories of compensation may strike us as implausible. As I have argued in the Introduction, however, we are scarcely entitled to dismiss the efforts of Dworkin, Ackerman, and others simply because their style of theorizing is extremely counterfactual. This is doubly the case given the amount of attention that these writers have lavished on the question of how their theories might be given practical application. In the next three chapters, then, I take these theorists seriously and try to engage them on their own terms. Only after making this effort will we be entitled to draw any general conclusions about the prospect of understanding social justice as a matter of the overall or inclusive claims of specific members of society.

Dworkin's Project

In order to understand the motivation behind Dworkin's rather complex description of equality of resources, it is best to begin by considering why he is critical of what has been called "equality of result."[3] Equality of result is a crude form of egalitarianism which demands that every person possess the same amount of material resources at every stage of one's life. According to Dworkin, the defect of equality of result is that it ignores the way in which each person's decisions about one's own life reduce or enhance the resources available for others. Supposing that we began from a situation of initially equal assets, some individuals would almost certainly consume their shares immediately, while others would contribute to the economy through their decisions to save, take risks, and make special efforts. Individuals whose choices and efforts contribute more to the lives of others thereby cost others less in collective resources. If equality requires that each be permitted over a lifetime to use no more than an equal share of the resources held in common, then we must take into consideration what has been consumed and contributed over time. These facts cannot be reflected unless individuals are allowed to hold unequal external assets. By insisting on strict material equality, equality of result ignores the fact that those who appear to be unequal may not be so, once their choices, sacrifices, and contributions are taken into account.

Dworkin's aim is to capture this more complex understanding of equality. For Dworkin, the value of a resource devoted to a single life must be assessed in terms of the cost of that resource to others. This cost must be measured in terms of the choices each person makes when confronted by the choices of others. Equality of resources therefore needs a special kind of metric, one that is sensitive to the effects of individual choice. As Dworkin puts it, any adequate metric of equality must be ambition-sensitive.[4]

Dworkin also assumes that talent should be counted as in some sense a part of each individual's resources. Since Dworkin does not believe that direct manipulation and transfer of mental and physical powers is compatible with integrity of the person, however, he asks how far differences in natural talent should influence the ownership of material assets.[5] Dworkin's view is that no one should have an unequal share of material resources simply because of an initially unequal distribution of talents. When this assumption is combined with the requirement that a metric of equality must be sensitive to the results of individual choice, the problem of establishing equality becomes one of devising a metric that is "ambition-sensitive," yet not "endowment-sensitive."[6] On this view, individuals can be deserving in virtue of their ambitions and efforts but not in virtue of their superior talents, since these should be counted as initial resources rather than as bases of personal desert.

Dworkin tries to devise a metric for equality in two stages. First, he proposes a thought-experiment in which we imagine a situation where talents and wealth are initially equal. In this imaginary situation, individuals hold an *auction* of all resources that can be held privately. The basic idea is that through this auction everyone is given an equal voice in determining the value of the resources that a society has on hand. The auction is a theoretical device for determining a set of holdings that remains perfectly equal when we view that set over the lifetimes of all members of society. In setting up the auction to yield this result, Dworkin tries to show us what complete equality would look like in principle.

The world in which Dworkin's auction takes place is rather unlike our own, however. For this reason, Dworkin proposes a second thought-experiment in which we imagine a hypothetical *insurance market*. The outcome of the insurance market is meant to approximate the outcome of the auction, but, unlike the results of the auction, Dworkin believes that we can translate the results of the insurance market into a set of redistributive taxes. In the hypothetical insurance market, individuals are first denied knowledge of the level of income their actual skills might allow them to earn. They are then offered insurance policies, on equal terms, against failing to have the skills that will produce whatever income they name. Given certain assumptions about attitudes toward risk, Dworkin then speculates about the way in which this insurance market would develop and the premium rate structure that would emerge. Finally, Dworkin suggests that we can set up a system of redistribution, modeled on this insurance market, by taxing individuals up to the limit of the premiums they would have paid under these hypothetical circumstances. The hypothetical insurance market is set up to give us standards for taxing the part of individual income that is due to talent rather than ambition, and through this redistributive tax scheme, equality in a world of unequal talents is approximately reestablished. This, in brief, is how Dworkin intends to show that equality in resources is a coherent and feasible ideal.

The Auction

To illustrate the idea of the auction, Dworkin tells a story about immigrants to a desert island who hit upon this device as a way of achieving equality in resources. Following Dworkin, then, imagine that individuals accept the accidents of raw material and technology that they find on their desert island, as well as the background distribution of the tastes they happen to have when they arrive. They ignore questions about the distribution of political power and the possibility of holding some resources in reserve for public use.[7] We are asked to assume that the immigrants possess equal talents, that is, they are "sufficiently equal in talent at the few modes of production that the resources allow so that each could produce roughly the same goods from the same set of resources."[8] Finally, immigrants to Dworkin's desert island are given an equal supply of tokens with which to bid on resources, and they are allowed to notify the auctioneer whenever they want to bid for some part of a resource as a distinct lot. Dworkin acknowledges that all of this is quite counterfactual and that the auction he imagines would be unworkably time-consuming. Nevertheless, we are to suppose that an auction is run until all markets clear. Because each person begins with an initially equal set of tokens, each person's bids play an equal part in determining the way in which resources are divided into bundles of goods and eventually allocated.[9]

There are two features of this initial auction that deserve special attention. First, Dworkin stipulates that participants in the auction have equal talents. Otherwise, once the auction is over and trade and production begin, individuals of superior talent will be able to command better occupations and more wealth and leisure than those who are not able to produce as much of what other people want. As mentioned, Dworkin assumes that tastes and ambitions are aspects of the person but that talents and abilities are part of a person's circumstances.[10] Since Dworkin assumes that justice demands full equality in resources over a lifetime, talents are therefore presumed to be equal.

The second important feature of the auction is that, in bidding on initial resources, individuals are bidding, indirectly, on the occupations they plan to engage in with the resources they end up securing. Unless initial bids in the auction can reflect what people intend to do with a particular resource in their future occupations, those bids cannot reflect the real value of that resource to the bidders over time; nor can the initial bid reflect, indirectly, the value that others place on productive purposes to which individuals plan to put their shares. In Dworkin's example, "Adrian" and "Bruce" both initially bid on a piece of land. According to Dworkin, the auction will fail to result in equality of resources "unless Adrian is able to bid a price for the same land that reflects his intention to work rather than play on it and so acquire whatever gain would prompt him to make that decision."[11] The profit that someone makes on a resource indirectly reflects, through the prices others are eventually willing to pay, the value that others place on having that resource (and those eventual profits). Of course, people may also want a resource, not for profit, but because they simply enjoy the occupation or the recreation that it permits them to have. This too must be reflected in the initial bids that individuals make.

In effect, the resources that individuals end up bidding on are three: material resources, occupations, and leisure time. We have just seen why occupations enter, indirectly, as one of the goods that are in effect purchased with initial tokens. But why does leisure time also figure as a resource? More generally, how does the auction commensurate the relative worth to each individual of different combinations of these three kinds of resources?

Although Dworkin does not make this clear, the key supposition in explaining how the auction works is, again, that talents for production are equal. This means that, on Dworkin's imaginary desert island, the production of goods *has a fixed cost in labor time.* Of course, individuals differ in the relative valuations that they place on leisure versus resources for consumption. But because for any individual, X amount of labor time always equals X amount of material resources, the trade-off between resources is objectively equivalent for everyone; in other words, there is a common metric for their valuations.

To illustrate, consider the range of possibilities that an initial bid can represent. At one extreme, people may plan to consume at leisure everything their initial bid purchases. At the other extreme, people's consumption may be minimal because they plan to put all of their time and initial resources into production. But whatever the choice, the total cost in resources to others of an individual's choices remains the same: if a person plans to lead a life of complete leisure one will have no more to consume than one's initial share commands. If one plans to produce, one will have more resources to consume as a result, but then must *sacrifice* an equivalent amount of time and effort for this additional consumption. The phrase "time is money" has a fixed meaning in the world Dworkin is imagining. Because the cost of producing resources is fixed and known in advance, initial resources can be allocated in a way that reflects their optimal use as defined through the auction.

Obviously, once we assume that talents are unequal it becomes impossible for initial bids to reflect different but equivalent individual evaluations of the relative worth of leisure, work, and consumption. Time spent in labor is no longer a fixed cost. Since some are more talented and therefore more productive than others, the fortunate few can have more of everything, even though they start with the same material assets. Not only is there unfairness, but it becomes impossible to determine the true value to others of any resource, since some individuals may have the same ambitions for a resource as others but not bid for it at all, given the competitive difficulty of making something out of that resource should they manage to secure it. Although the reason that Dworkin gives for assuming that talents are equal is one of justice, he might as well have said that the reason for assuming that talents are equal is to provide a common measure of the relative value of resources to each person. Only if production costs are fixed can the bids that individuals make reflect different but commensurate valuations of consumption, work, and leisure time.

Given these special features, Dworkin believes that the auction leads to perfect equality in resources over a lifetime. Of course, after the initial auction of resources is concluded and trade and production are in progress, it may appear to the casual observer that individuals have in fact become very unequal. But we must remember that those who appear to have more than others have also had to expend more time and effort than others in acquiring what they now possess. The purpose of the auction is to take into the balance all of the possible costs and contributions that people can make over a lifetime and have them all come out equal. By fixing the amount of time that each person must spend in order to produce further resources for consumption or production, Dworkin believes that the auction achieves a situation of complete equality. It does so because each person begins with an initial set of preferences for work, consumption, and leisure but must then revise these preferences in response to the preferences of others through a process of competitive bidding. Each person ends up with a bundle of goods that no one else can legitmately envy because each has done as well as possible given the preferences of others. The point of the auction is that "people decide what sorts of lives to pursue against a background of information about the actual cost that their choices impose on other people and hence on the total stock of resources that may be fairly used by them."[12] Or, as Dworkin explains in another passage: "The market character of the auction is not simply a convenient or *ad hoc* device for resolving technical problems. . . . It is an institutionalized form of the process of discovery and adaptation which is at the center of equality of resources."[13] By assuming that talents are equal, the auction offers a metric of equality that is sensitive only to differences in ambition.

Of course, Dworkin recognizes that this theoretical device for explaining what equality of resources consists in is too counterfactual to be of any practical use. This becomes apparent when he asks how we could neutralize the role played by different talents under actual circumstances. Any tax scheme for redistributing resources modeled directly on the auction would have to be a compromise in which we tried to tax that component of wealth due to talent but left alone that component of wealth due to ambition.[14] Under actual circumstances, however, talent and ambition cannot be distinguished; they interact from the beginning in determining what individuals choose to be and do. It is impossible to say counterfactually what a world of equal talents would look like. We would have to "decide what sort and level of talent each person had and what income individuals would reach exploiting the same talents to different degrees," and this is impossible.[15] Dworkin therefore turns to another thought-experiment, the hypothetical insurance market.

We should pause here to ask whether Dworkin has identified the central reason why his theoretical description of equality in resources cannot be used. Dworkin locates the major stumbling block in our inability to imagine a world of equal talents. But even supposing we could specify such a world, we might still wonder if the auction described so far makes any sense. Indeed, the entire process looks circular in a way reminiscent of our discussion in the last chapter of the problem of specifying initial holdings. Recall that in Chapter 2 I argue that we cannot regard economic contribution as a fundamental principle of social justice because we must first specify initial holdings on separate grounds. A similar sort of objection seems to apply here. Unlike an ordinary market, the auction requires that everyone be able to *foresee* what will happen when the auction is over and trade and production begin. This foresight is required because the future use of resources must be part of the motivation for bidding on resources. To know the true value of a resource *over a lifetime*, we must already know what price resources will bring, that is, what individuals will be willing to pay for the goods they can produce with their initial shares. But we do not know what individuals will pay until the auction is already concluded and people begin to use their assets (and change their minds). Rather than expressing an ongoing "process of adaptation and discovery," the auction that Dworkin describes requires that individuals be prescient. The auction is therefore impossible even given a world of equal talents. For the auction to run successfully, it is not enough for individuals to know what others actually bid and to revise their own bids accordingly; rather, they must also know what those bids augur for the future before they can revise their own intentions in a way that will preserve equality once trade and production begin. To put the same point in another way, participants in the auction must be able to anticipate what everyone else will do with their initial shares in order to know whether the resources that they bid on will eventually be worth what they hope. But everyone in the initial auction that Dworkin describes is in the same position: they do not know whether there will in fact be a market for their projects until assets are distributed and trade and production begin. Unless they can forecast the results of production and exchange in advance, they do not know the value of the resources they are actually bidding on. Although Dworkin's idea of an auction in resources is ingenious, it does not even in principle yield a set of equal holdings over a lifetime. It is incoherent unless we suppose a certain clairvoyance on the part of the participants.[16]

The Insurance Market

Even though Dworkin does not mention the difficulties above, he does recognize that for other reasons the auction has serious difficulties as the basis of a redistributive tax. He therefore turns next to the notion of a hypothetical insurance market that offers coverage against failing to have *skills* that will command a high income. The idea of an insurance market appeals to Dworkin for two reasons. First, this device again allows each person to play an equal role in determining the value of resources, since individual ambition supposedly settles the question of how much insurance each individual will buy. Second, the device of an insurance market promises a definite set of solutions to questions about the amounts and kinds of compensation due to specific individuals. These advantages can be illustrated through the notion of insurance against certain kinds of *handicaps*. Traditionally, the problem presented by handicaps and special medical needs lies in setting the upper bounds of compensation. How much income, for example, is enough to make up for the fact that someone is born a quadraplegic? What is the normal standard of health that serves as a benchmark of compensation in deciding how much physical therapy is due a stroke victim? As Charles Fried has observed, under conditions of moderate scarcity, special needs may become voracious, requiring transfer payments that would lower aggregate welfare to intolerable levels. The advantage of insurance is that it allows the market to decide which handicaps should be compensated and to what extent, while avoiding the problems of interpersonal comparisons of welfare and the specification of normal powers. By making compensation dependent on private decisions about the risks that individuals are willing to bear, the market both specifies and limits the amount due when the handicap that was insured against occurs.[17]

By treating the failure to have certain *skills* as, in effect, a certain kind of *handicap*, Dworkin hopes to capitalize on the general advantages of insurance as a solution to problems of individual compensation. In the hypothetical insurance market, individuals are placed in a situation of ignorance about their actual circumstances. Rather than distinguishing the results of luck and ambition directly, the hypothetical insurance market will offer each person the same gambles on the income one might turn out to be able to command once Dworkin's own version of Rawls's veil of ignorance is lifted. The insurance market on skills is, of course, structured by the general way in which most individuals balance the value of income against the various costs they must pay if they lose their insurance bet. But the market gives everyone an equal chance when facing the natural and social lottery. Everyone has the same risk of turning out not to have certain abilities (which serve as the basis for developing a range of skills), and everyone has the same opportunity to insure against such eventualities.

At this point, the easiest way to understand the idea of an insurance market is by summarizing Dworkin's speculations about how it might actually work. Imagine, then, that individuals know their own skills and ambitions, as well as the income structure of their society, but are quite in the dark about what income their own skills might allow them to generate. Insurance is offered against failing to have whatever income an individual names, with insurance companies paying the difference between the coverage level that is initially chosen and the income that individuals in fact turn out to be able to earn.[18] Dworkin then asks what sort of insurance rate structure might develop under such circumstances. Would everyone buy such high levels of coverage as to make it unlikely that anyone would sell insurance?

The first feature to note about this hypothetical market is that individuals are unlikely to turn out to have the skills necessary to earn a very high income. Insurance companies are therefore likely to lose on policies guaranteeing a high income and will structure their rates accordingly. To cover their potential losses, the cost of such coverage will be high. As a result, the financial benefit of qualifying for compensation will be low, given the premiums that the insuree has agreed to in advance and will now have to meet. Such insurance is a "financially disadvantageous bet." However, the key feature of coverage at a high level of income is that it is not only a bad financial gamble on future welfare but possibly a catastrophic one, assuming the declining marginal utility of money. This is because a person who fails to qualify for compensation—that is, turns out to have the talent necessary to earn a large income—must almost certainly have to work at close to maximum earning capacity just to pay off the premiums. Not only will the insurees have to work extremely hard; they will also in all probability forfeit a great deal of freedom in their choice of occupations. Few people will turn out to be so talented that they can qualify for more than a few high-paying jobs. And, as Dworkin points out, almost no one wishes to be enslaved by their potential earning power in this way.[19] Given the premiums that are likely to be in effect and the cost in welfare of failing to qualify for compensation, few persons will insure against failing to command great wealth. The insurance market that Dworkin proposes will not prove unworkable by turning out to guarantee everyone vast amounts of money.[20]

We now come to the second key feature of the market. As the chosen level of coverage declines,

> the odds that any particular person will have the talents necessary to earn that income improve, and for a substantial section of income levels in normal economies, improve faster than the rate of that decline. Many more than twice as many people have the abilities necessary to earn the amount earned in the fiftieth percentile than in the ninety-ninth percentile of a normal income distribution. So the premium falls, and falls, at least over a considerable range, at a rate faster than the rate of the coverage.[21]

At relatively low rates of coverage, almost everyone would be able to choose among a wide range of occupations, any one of which would allow them to pay off their premiums while still retaining significant leisure and income for consumption. Dworkin argues that we can choose an average coverage level generated by this hypothetical market and translate the premium paid on that level of coverage into a tax, to be redistributed to those who do not have the ability to earn at that level. Finally, individuals buying insurance under the stipulated conditions of uncertainty could increase their expected welfare if they bought insurance fixed as a percentage of what they in fact turned out to earn rather than at a flat rate. This allows Dworkin to suggest some form of graduated income tax as the best way of approximating equality of resources.[22]

The above exercise is speculative in a number of damaging ways, but before looking at the difficulties, I wish to underscore the implicit assumptions that explain why Dworkin thinks we might find the insurance market plausible and attractive. Dworkin assumes what might be called a "normal range of ambition." There is some standard combination of leisure, work, and consumption (or range of combinations) with which most individuals are content: few individuals are willing to make great sacrifices for wealth and few are completely indifferent toward being wealthy. If ambition alone explained the distribution of income, we would therefore expect that the distribution of income would fall roughly along a bell-shaped curve. That is, with talents equal, the number of individuals willing to sacrifice great amounts of leisure for wealth, and vice versa, would ordinarily be rather small, since individuals' ambitions normally do not run to either of these extremes. Assuming roughly similar ambitions, then, deviations from this bell-shaped distribution under actual circumstances must be explained in terms of "luck" (i.e., natural and social contingencies). In other words, the reason that under actual circumstances more people command higher (or lower) incomes than we might otherwise expect is not because they are more (or less) ambitious but because they are luckier, that is, they began with greater unearned advantages, such as special natural talents that allowed them to develop scarce and highly demanded skills.

The insurance-tax scheme is a way of allowing everyone to share the same chance of turning out to be lucky, thereby evening out the effects of chance. The notion of a normal range of ambition is expressed in Dworkin's argument through his assumption that insurees have roughly the same declining marginal utility from income. After a certain point the possibility of commanding a high income begins to pale next to the possibility of losing other sources of welfare, such as leisure time.

Of course, neither Dworkin nor anyone else really knows exactly what sort of premium rate structure would develop in the market he imagines. These are speculations about the sort of behavior that seems generally likely under conditions of uncertainty; and, of course, we cannot literally carry out this thought-experiment. However, Dworkin supposes that members of a society governed by equality of resources could assign the task of predicting the results of an insurance market to a computer:

> before the initial auction begins, information about the tastes, talents, and attitudes towards risk of each individual, as well as information about the raw materials and technology available, is delivered to a computer. It then predicts not only the results of the auction but the projected income structure. . . . The computer is then asked another hypothetical question . . . [Given the conditions of the market] how much of such insurance would individuals, on average, buy, and at what cost?[23]

Leaving aside the fact that a computer could not run an initial auction of resources for the reasons discussed in the last section, it is now time to ask whether Dworkin's own speculations about how the insurance market might operate can provide a sound basis for redistributive policies. The first question is whether Dworkin's speculations about the insurance scheme mirror in any way the theoretical ideal he described earlier. Recall that the purpose of Dworkin's exercise is to provide a standard for approximating equality in resources on a person-by-person basis. To do so he must provide a metric that is sensitive to individual valuations of consumption, occupation, and leisure.

We should note first that, unlike the initial auction, individuals in Dworkin's imaginary insurance market do not make choices in light of their preferences for an *occupation* of a particular sort. Instead, the problem that Dworkin poses in the insurance market is purely one of taking a risk on *income* under conditions of uncertainty. It is difficult to see how vocational ambitions enter into the decision at all, given that the problem is one of turning out to have a certain chosen income no matter what particular occupation a person turns out to have. The initial device of the auction is at least sensitive to a desire for meaningful work, by balancing the value of having a particular occupation against other particular goods. In the insurance market, however, individuals balance expected income against some degree of freedom in choosing among occupations. Information about the *particular* ambitions and tastes of individuals is therefore irrelevant, even if we possessed such information and could program it into Dworkin's computer. To this extent the insurance market is basically insensitive to ambition and fails to reflect the aim of equality in resources.

Of course, in the insurance market individuals can still choose from a range of occupations, given an insurance policy with a low enough premium, so perhaps this problem is not a serious one. But Dworkin's insurance scheme is insensitive to individual ambition in other ways as well. Dworkin acknowledges that the insurance market must treat skills as purely a matter of luck and therefore must ignore the way in which individuals choose to *develop* some talents rather than others. Statistical discrimination against those whose high income is due to hard work and ambition rather than talent is thus inevitable, although Dworkin thinks this is acceptable.[24] Such discrimination will occur because the insurance market is a compromise: it assumes that the higher the income the greater the role of natural and social contingencies in general, while admitting that this is not always true of particular individuals. For this reason the insurance scheme is most plausible at the lower end of the income scale. In other words, it seems reasonable to think that, below some (necessarily speculative) level of income, coverage would indeed be purchased by practically everyone under the conditions Dworkin describes. We can assume that practically everyone has the ambition for at least some income during their life. But as the level of coverage increases, the bargain represented by insurance depends more and more upon facts not specified, particularly on the exact distribution of talent and ambition in a given society. For example, it may be the case that many individuals care less about their relative freedom to choose their occupation than Dworkin believes. This might be because people simply care about income itself rather than occupation, or worry about providing for their children, or wish for the status associated with income, or are interested in wealth for some other combination of reasons. None of these possibilities are implausible, but nothing hangs on any one of them being correct. The point is that Dworkin must guess at complex cultural attitudes toward the family, wealth, and occupation in order for his computer to model current ambitions, especially in trying to set higher levels of taxation. Otherwise the market again fails to reflect individual ambition accurately. But any speculation about these attitudes is bound to be controversial.

Finally, any actual distribution of income reflects an indeterminate mix of talent and ambition, as I note in my explanation of why unequal talents make the initial auction both unfair and indeterminate in result. However, the distribution of income in any actual society reflects a much more complex set of factors than is accounted for in Dworkin's model. As noted in the last chapter, any existing income structure reflects the arrangement of an entire system of production, including property and inheritance laws, decisions about efficiency and the production of public goods, expenditures on national defense, and so on. Presumably, we must modify some of these arrangements and retain others in seeking to make society more just. We cannot, however, realistically regard any actual distribution of income as the result of only two sources, legitimate ambition and illegitimate talent or luck (a catchall category). Any explanation of why individuals currently have what they do must be much more complex than this and take into account decisions about matters like efficiency, which already influence the holdings which individuals possess. Yet, Dworkin's scheme must begin with hypothetical insurees taking *some* income structure as the basis of their probabilistic calculations about how much insurance to buy. Which income structure do they begin with?

At this point the deep incoherence of Dworkin's project becomes apparent again, for Dworkin bases the insurance market on the income structure produced (via computer) in the initial auction. But, as I point out, in order for the initial auction to be successful, we must assume that talents are *already* equal and that those participating in the auction can already *foresee* the income structure that will result once trade and production begin. In other words, the insurance market is either superfluous or impossible. The insurance market is superfluous if we can hold the auction because in this case the auction already insures equality over time. The insurance market is impossible if we cannot hold the auction, because in this case the insurance market presupposes that trade and production have occurred—and this presupposes, in turn, that we begin from some *initial* distribution of income that is already fair. Without running the auction, however, we have no idea whether the income structure we begin with is fair or not. For this reason, then, neither part of Dworkin's description of equality in resources makes sense.

To all of this it might be replied that in calculating how much insurance people are likely to buy we are simply to start from the present income structure of our society. After all, the insurance market scheme is intended to be the basis of redistributive policies in our world. The trouble with this response is that it simply ignores the point that any actual distribution of income already reflects a much more complicated set of factors than Dworkin's model allows. By taking the income structure of our own society as a basis of calculation, Dworkin is in effect asking us to treat modern industrial economies in the same way we might treat a "desert island" economy for the purpose of deciding a fair rate of taxation. He must proceed in this way in order to avoid all of the complications just raised.

But surely this begs the question of the influence of the basic structure on all individual holdings. Why should we take the present income structure or any projected income structure as the basis for calculations about what insurance we ought to buy in a hypothetical market? The income structure of any actual society was not produced by initial auction of resources, could not be produced by such an auction, and in any event already reflects a great number of additional influences on the distribution of income that we cannot ignore.

Our conclusion must be that, despite the sophistication and ingenuity of Dworkin's argument, his attempt to devise a metric for assessing individual claims to overall equality only reveals how difficult the project is both theoretically and practically. It is, of course, to Dworkin's credit that he recognizes most of the problems involved in such a project and presents a view of equality that is far from the crude equalitarianism of "equality of result." But even in Dworkin's account, we are required as a matter of "ideal theory" to disentangle the effects of personal effort and circumstance over a lifetime and in advance of any transactions; and at the practical level, we must base our decisions on a hypothetical insurance market that takes the very thing that is in question, namely, the income structure of society, as a basis of calculation. Even if we could somehow waive this problem, the hypothetical insurance market nevertheless remains insensitive to individual ambition in a variety of ways and depends for its implementation on a number of controversial assumptions about the attitudes that individuals have toward work, consumption, and leisure. The very failure of Dworkin's metric of equality shows the full magnitude of the task that has been undertaken. It also illustrates quite clearly why Rawls thinks that we must shift our attention to the basic structure and treat the question that Dworkin raises as unanswerable in principle.

Dworkin is hardly the only philosopher who has tried to develop a theory of social justice that focuses on the overall claims of specific individuals. We cannot conclude that Rawls is right about the impossibility of this task, therefore, without looking at other recent attempts to carry this project through. The next logical theory to examine is the one presented by Bruce Ackerman. For as Dworkin points out, there are at least two kinds of "liberalism."[25] Dworkin's brand of liberalism assumes that the basic requirement of social justice is equality. It argues that the state should be neutral in matters of personal morality because forcing individuals to live according to a particular conception of the good is incompatible with treating them with equal concern and respect.

The other brand of liberalism is Ackerman's, which reverses this relation between equality and neutrality: neutrality toward particular conceptions of the good is assumed to be the basic standard of a liberal theory of social justice, and equality follows only to the extent that neutrality requires it.

It is doubtful whether either moral theory is adequate, and for this reason I will also consider William Galston's perfectionist theory of justice in Chapter 5. But the philosophical adequacy of first principles are not my major concern in this book. The primary reason I now turn to Ackerman's theory is that this second brand of liberalism demands a less encompassing sort of equality than the first. Ackerman's theory would also seem to require a simpler metric of equality for redressing the situations of particular individuals. In short, by starting from a set of different first principles, Ackerman may be able to succeed where Dworkin fails.

NOTES

1. Dworkin's criticisms of equality in welfare focus on what sort of preferences should be allowed to count when our object is to make people equal in their "overall success" in life. Dworkin argues that we must rely on the notion of "reasonable regret" about the opportunities some people are denied in order to make sense of the complaint that some people were deprived of an equal chance at overall success. The notion of reasonable regret, however, already presupposes ideas of fairness and equality in resources. See "Equality of Welfare," pp. 185-247.

2. Dworkin assumes that some deep form of substantive equality is a basic requirement of social justice. While this matter lies outside the scope of this book, I should at least note why this assumption is problematic. In Part 2 of "What Is Equality," Dworkin says that the ideal of equality in resources is necessary to explain why the original position is a useful device for considering what justice is, and he refers to an earlier essay in *Taking Rights Seriously* that supposedly shows why "the force of the original position depends on the adequacy of an interpretation of equality in resources and not vice versa" (p. 345). But what Dworkin's earlier essay argues is that the force of the original position depends on a much more abstract principle of "equal concern and respect." The connection between this abstract principle and any particular substantive requirement of equality is never established, only asserted; and, of course, many critics of Dworkin have argued that his formal principle of equal concern and respect is in fact compatible with a wide range of substantive principles, including some that recommend various kinds of deep-going substantive inequalities. If these criticisms are sound (as I believe they are), then we have reason for questioning Dworkin's project before it ever gets off the ground. As I have stressed, however, these matters are outside our main

concern. For this criticism of Dworkin, see Hart, "Between Utility and Rights," pp. 821-46; Flathman, "Equality and Generalization," pp. 38-61.

3. For Dworkin's explanation of "equality of result" see "Why Liberals Should Believe in Equality," p. 32.

4. Dworkin, "Equality of Resources," p. 311.

5. Ibid., p. 301.

6. Ibid., p. 311.

7. Dworkin's decision to set aside questions about which resources should be held publicly leaves some of the most important problems of social justice unresolved. Similarly, his decision to accept market preferences as a measure of value is problematic for the reasons given in Chapter 2. For a more extensive discussion of these issues, see Bennet, "Ethics and Markets," pp. 195-205.

8. Dworkin, "Equality of Resources," p. 288.

9. Ibid., pp. 285-86.

10. Ibid., p. 302.

11. Ibid., p. 305.

12. Ibid., p. 289.

13. Ibid., p. 314.

14. Ibid., p. 313.

15. Ibid., p. 316.

16. At this point, it might be replied that individuals do not need to know what will happen in the future; instead, they simply make the best probabilistic guess they can on the basis of current information. It should be remembered, however, that the auction is supposed to be "an institutionalized form of the process of discovery and adaptation which is at the center of equality of resources" (Ibid., p. 289). In guessing about the future, no such discovery and adaptation takes place. If individuals guess badly about what their resources will eventually be worth to others, subsequent market transactions will not correct this mistake, and they will continue to envy the initial resources that others have.

17. Ibid., pp. 292-304.

18. Ibid., pp. 314-19.

19. Ibid., p. 322.

20. Ibid., p. 321.

21. Ibid.

22. Ibid., pp. 323-26.

23. Ibid., p. 317.

24. Ibid., pp. 315, 328.

25. Dworkin, "What Liberalism Isn't," p. 47. Dworkin attacks Ackerman's neutrality principle on the grounds that it confuses liberal neutrality in matters of personal morality with neutrality toward public conceptions of justice. According to Dworkin, the first kind of neutrality is required by a *nonneutral* liberal principle of equality. Whether Ackerman's theory is "liberal" or not, however, the more important questions are whether Ackerman can provide a neutral justification for principles of justice and, if he can, why such a justification should be preferred. Dworkin and Ackerman both occasionally men-

tion fear of authority, qualified moral skepticism, and the ideal of autonomy as reasons why liberals have traditionally emphasized the importance of limited government. But neither theorist spends much time examining these (more plausible) historical bases of liberalism. In any case, liberalism may neither have nor need some single principle as its foundation.

CHAPTER 4

Ackerman on Initial Equality in Resources

Turning from Ronald Dworkin to Bruce Ackerman, our main concern remains the same. We are still interested in how recent theorists of social justice have tried to overcome the problems identified in Chapter 2 by developing a workable metric for commensurating individual claims of redress. Ackerman's purpose is broader than Dworkin's, however, since he is not concerned exclusively with describing a complex principle of equality. Ackerman's *Social Justice and the Liberal State* aims instead at defending a particular version of liberalism. Ackerman believes that the distinctive mark of liberalism is neutrality toward particular conceptions of the good. Of course, many theorists argue that it is impossible for the state to maintain this sort of neutrality. But Ackerman thinks that a liberal conception of the state can be vindicated by showing that we can justify an activist egalitarian social policy even though beginning from a situation that ensures strict neutrality.

Ackerman develops his theory in three stages. At the stage of ideal theory we encounter yet another imaginary-choice situation. This time we are treated to a group of pioneers about to colonize a planet. (Although I will pay little attention to the counterfactual details of this exercise, it must at least be sketched in order to give an idea of how the argument proceeds.) Ackerman writes various scripts or "neutral dialogues" which take place among these pioneers on the subject of how their new planet should be organized. Their conversational endeavor is to find a set of distributive principles that passes the test of neutrality. Their problem is radically simplified in various ways. The only resource they must initially divide is a perfectly fungible stuff called "manna," which they find conveniently waiting for them. Ackerman's pioneers also have transmitter-shields that allow costless negotiation and transaction once trade and production begin. Finally, the pioneers possess a perfect science of eugenics.

Against this background, Ackerman's imaginary pioneers begin by discussing the problem of dividing their common stock of manna. They go on to debate virtually every topic within the theory of justice, from eugenics to the role of liberal education. After completing this task at the level of ideal theory, Ackerman next considers how ideal rights to initial equality might be realized as matters of second-best theory.[1] Under second-best conditions, the assumptions concerning manna and a perfect technology of justice are dropped, although it is still assumed that individuals are motivated to comply with whatever principles of justice are chosen. In making second-best adjustments to the imperfections of actual society, Ackerman argues that neutrality requires that each person sacrifice no more than an equal share of ideal rights. Because neutrality forbids the ranking of resources according to any particular conception of the good, Ackerman's second-best theory faces the difficult task of showing what an 'equal' sacrifice of rights might consist of under these conditions.[2]

What is of specific interest for us in Ackerman's theory is the promise it seems to hold for overcoming some of the difficulties that plagued Dworkin's account of equality. Dworkin aimed at a description of equality of resources, person by person, over a lifetime. Ackerman aims instead at a description of initial equality in resources. This is an important change in how the notion of redress is understood. With Ackerman, the principle of redress now becomes in one respect what Dworkin has called a "starting gate" principle: handicaps are compensated so that each may start out even in a fair race, but once there has been a fair start individual holdings are allowed to develop over time through free transactions.[3] This avoids the problem that Dworkin had to deal with, that is, determining in advance how trade and production will affect individual holdings. Obviously, it is of some interest whether this more restricted understanding of equality can succeed where Dworkin's principle failed. By leaving it to the market to settle the question of individual holdings once trade and production begin, Ackerman, unlike Dworkin, accepts some of the limits on allocative justice discussed in Chapter 2. He does not try to keep track of an endless variety of changing relative positions in order to compensate individuals for what they would have had if only they could have foreseen the choices of others. Nevertheless, Ackerman does try to deal with the basic problem of how assets should be initially distributed. He does so by trying to justify, on strictly neutral grounds, a particular starting point for free transactions.

In this light, our major interest is in Ackerman's justification of the principle of initial equality and his attempt to give that principle concrete application under second-best conditions. Coincidentally, these issues are also the main subject of Ackerman's commentators. Practically everyone who has written on Ackerman challenges the neutral justification of his basic principle. I will argue, however, that this part of Ackerman's theory is in fact successful. My own criticism is somewhat different: Ackerman's success at the level of ideal theory is exactly the reason for his failure at the level of second- and third-best theory. In order to provide a neutral justification for initial equality in his pioneers' manna, he must argue for a simple arithmetical division of resources, on the grounds that any other division of resources would require controversial cardinal comparisons of interpersonal welfare. Ackerman can argue that an equal division of manna avoids this requirement because manna is an all-purpose, infinitely fungible resource. However, under actual circumstances we do not have any manna. Instead, we must assess the relative importance of many competing resources, and this necessitates controversial cardinal judgments of welfare that Ackerman's theory forbids in principle. In short, Ackerman's argument at the level of ideal theory makes it logically impossible to solve actual problems of distribution once his initial assumptions about the circumstances of justice are dropped.

Ackerman's Justification of Initial Equality

As stated, Ackerman's argument takes place through a series of imaginary dialogues about candidate principles of justice. These dialogues are governed by "conversational constraints" that require neutrality toward particular conceptions of the good. Ackerman's conversational constraints consist broadly in the following three rules:

Rationality. Whenever anybody questions the legitimacy of another's claim, the claimant must respond not by suppressing the questioner but by giving a reason that explains why the claimant is more entitled to the resource than the questioner is.[4]

Consistency. The reason advanced by a claimant on one occasion must not be inconsistent with the reasons advanced to justify other claims.[5]

Neutrality. No reason is a good reason if it requires the claimant to assert: (a) that his conception of the good is better than any of those asserted by his fellow citizens, or (b) that, regardless of his conception of the good, he is intrinsically superior to one or more of his fellow citizens.[6] In order to pass the test of neutral dialogue, any argument for a proposed rule of distribution must satisfy these criteria. The rationality criterion is actually a bit more involved than its statement above, but the only additional feature we need to note here is the requirement of "comprehensiveness," which means simply that any proposed rule of distribution must be shown to be preferable to all of its alternatives. Obviously, the neutrality criterion does most of the work in this scheme. Ackerman refers to clause (a) of that criterion as a ban against "selectivity" and to clause (b) as a ban against assertions of "unconditional superiority." In addition, he also assumes that no "historical" right or "legitimate expectation" can be used to show that one person deserves more than another: all distributive rights must emerge as the result of conversations that pass the test of neutral dialogue. Since Ackerman assumes that all rights must emerge as the result of dialogue itself, his argument is directed primarily at consequentialist attempts to pass neutrality. In fact, he confines his discussion to two doctrines, hedonistic utilitarianism and something he calls the principle of "equal fulfillment." For our purposes, only the latter principle is important, since we hardly need to review the argument that shows that choosing to measure the good in terms of psychological sensation or "pleasure" is nonneutral with respect to the other ways in which fulfillment might be assessed.

What Ackerman calls the "principle of equal fulfillment" is the crucial test of his argument, for it is a consequentialist principle that clearly seems to be completely neutral toward particular conceptions of the good. The principle of equal fulfillment requires that resources be divided so that each can get an "equal distance" toward realizing their goals, or, alternatively, so that each person can have an "equal chance" at realizing their goals. Ackerman considers "equal fulfillment" in either version a crucial test because this principle seems to require neither an assertion of the "unconditional superiority" of one conception of the good over all others nor an assessment of the content of particular conceptions of the good. What is proposed is simply that resources be allocated so that individuals get an equal distance toward their goals, whatever those goals happen to be.

Ackerman attacks equal fulfillment on the basis that such a principle can only make sense "in terms of life-plans that have a particular shape to them. . . . Its partisans imagine that all of us conceive the good life as if we were mountaineers intent upon a slow and steady ascent to some high perch that signifies final victory. It is only in this mountaineering metaphor the we can speak of two people getting 'halfway toward their ultimate ends.' "[7] As counterexamples, Ackerman introduces two characters, "Jumper" and "Struggler," who demand to know why this particular metric for measuring fulfillment should be used. Jumper has goals that are discontinuous; success is an all-or-nothing matter, rather than a matter of the *degree* to which his goals or preferences are fulfilled. Struggler constantly sets himself new goals upon fulfilling earlier ones. Neither conception of success can be accommodated within the notion of equal fulfillment without some further justification of the metric used for measuring equal fulfillment. According to Ackerman, any metric proposed must itself be justified in a way that violates neutrality.

The argument Ackerman makes in his dialogue on equal fulfillment has been obscure to many of his critics. Therefore, before I consider some criticisms of that argument, it will be helpful to consider just what Ackerman is driving at when he introduces imaginary characters who measure fulfillment in different ways. His point is actually very simple: any metric for measuring equality along one dimension of value, such as fulfillment, precludes the use of other metrics. Consider a principle that Ackerman does not explicitly discuss: equality in the satisfaction of preferences. If we decide to measure equality by counting preferences that have been satisfied, this precludes measuring equality in terms of success in reaching a single dominant preference. Measurement in terms of a dominant goal in turn precludes measurement in terms of discontinuous or changing goals, each of which might be weighted differently by individuals. And measurement in terms of "states of consciousness" obviously precludes all of the metrics above.

It is true that each of the metrics just mentioned is indifferent to the content of a wide range of life plans—those that implicitly reckon success by the metric in question. None of these metrics is completely neutral, however; and choosing one metric necessarily excludes others, which are integral to the self-understandings of some individuals, for example, Jumper and Struggler. To justify a metric by the rationality criteria means giving a neutral reason for it, but there seems to be no way of picking out one metric and excluding others without insisting that the metric chosen is superior because it counts what should really matter to individuals. Ackerman concludes: "We search in vain for a neutral yard-stick for measuring the 'real' value of different conceptions of the good. To justify one yard-stick over all the other possible ways of ranking values will require utterances that are inconsistent with at least some of the ideals affirmed by some of your fellow citizens."[8]

The importance of this dialogue will become clear once we turn to Ackerman's solution. How does he hope to give a neutral justification for any distribution rule, given the strict interpretation of neutrality just revealed? His solution is to abandon the search for a neutral metric of value. In other words, Ackerman gives up the project of trying to divide manna so that shares are proportional to a division along some further dimension of value. Instead, he proposes an arithmetic division of manna into initially equal shares. Arithmetic equality satisfies the rationality constraint because there is something to be said on its behalf: "regardless of his conception of the good, each citizen deserves manna simply because he has identified himself as a purposive being willing to affirm *some* conception of the good."[9] Of course, this rationale for dividing resources is still deficient, as Ackerman recognizes, since it only says that each should get some resources without saying how much. Neutrality also permits each of us to say, "I am at least as good as you are," and therefore "I should get at least as much of this stuff that both of us desire."[10] This key assertion, repeated endlessly in Ackerman's theory, does not specify *how much* value any person or plan of life has. Its apparent attraction is that it involves no assertion of superiority or evaluation of life plans. Using this rationale, a principle of equality does emerge from neutral dialogue. It has a very weak justification: something can be said on its behalf, it survives the test of neutrality, and it allows interlocutors to reach agreement. Initial equality simply "falls out" of neutral conversation as the only solution that does not defeat itself by positing yet another yardstick of the "real" value of resources. To summarize Ackerman's argument:

> 1) I am a person with a conception of the good.
> 2) Simply by virtue of being such a person, I'm at least as good as you are.
> 3) This is reason enough for me to get as much manna as you do—as long as you have nothing more to say that will neutrally justify a claim to additional manna.[11]

The most economical way to amplify Ackerman's argument at this point is by considering why various criticisms of it misfire. There are three basic criticisms: (1) Ackerman's argument against the principle of equal fulfillment fails; (2) there are other principles that pass neutrality besides arithmetical equality; and (3) Ackerman's own principle fails neutrality. J. L. Mackie makes the first two criticisms:

> Ackerman's arguments against the principle of equal fulfillment are unsound. He says that if [equal fulfillment] yields an unequal distribution, anyone can protest, "so the only thing that prevents one from getting the manna is the character of my ideals." Though this is literally true, it does *not* mean that part (a) of the neutrality constraint is violated. Though our claimant gets less because of what his ideals are, it is not because they are being held to be inferior. Ackerman here is guilty of a blatant fallacy in the use of his own constraints.[12]

Mackie also argues that another principle passes the neutrality test: "It would not be easy to dismiss the utilitarianism that identifies utility with the satisfaction of preferences. . . . The satisfaction of preferences is not a particular conception of the good, but the general form of any such conception."[13] Other critics, such as Fishkin, agree with this latter criticism: "Equal satisfaction in the utilitarian sense should be distinguished from another criterion that Ackerman calls 'equal fulfillment'. . . . If I claim only that I should be *as satisfied* with my share as you are with yours, it is hard to see how that would amount to a claim that 'my conception of the good is better.' "[14]

The problem with all of these criticisms is the same. To begin with, Ackerman admits at the outset that equal fulfillment does not require us to judge a person's conception of the good; that is why the principle is regarded as a crucial test. The principle of equal fulfillment passes neutrality, but the difficulty is that the metric used by the principle must itself be justified according to the rationality constraint, and no metric, whether for equal fulfillment or equal satisfaction, can itself be justified on neutral grounds. To claim, as Mackie does, that one kind of metric, like the equal satisfaction of preferences, is "the general form of any particular conception of the good" ignores the sort of challenge that Ackerman explicitly raises in the dialogue on equal fulfillment. The thrust of that dialogue is that individuals disagree about how to measure success or welfare in the first place and that this disagreement reflects their disparate visions of what is really worthwhile in life. Mackie's (and Fishkin's) arguments are directed at violations of neutrality at the wrong level of generality. They focus on supposed violations of neutrality toward particular conceptions of the good. But the point is that any particular conception of the good presupposes a general metric for measuring success and failure in realizing the good, and these general metrics are both implied in particular conceptions of the good and necessarily controversial. As long as there can be different ways of calculating personal success, no method of calculation can be neutral.

The natural objection at this point is that Ackerman's criteria of neutrality are so strict that no distributive rule can pass them, including Ackerman's own principle. As Fishkin puts it, "Only if equal amounts of manna were assumed, at the outset, to be the appropriate criteria for judging that people are equally well-off would it follow that differing distributions yielding equal utilities were a slight to some conceptions of the good."[15] But this objection again misunderstands the argument. Neutrality does not aim at making persons equally well-off or at any particular outcome; nor is it denied that any neutral rule, including Ackerman's principle, will inevitably make some worse off in some conceptions of welfare. As Ackerman stresses, "Neutrality is *not* a characteristic of the *outcome* of a decision rule; instead, it is a feature of the *conversation* through which a distribution rule is justified."[16]

I have argued that neutrality in effect stipulates that no rule of distribution can involve a metric that is itself nonneutral. The arithmetic rule of initial equality satisfies this stipulation because it does not seek to make individuals equal along another particular dimension of value; rather, it seeks to make them equal in the possession of resources that have *some* value for individual life plans, no matter how those plans reckon success. The rule only requires ordinal judgments to the effect that more manna is better than some and some is better than none, but it does not require cardinal judgments about how much better off a person would be with more resources. Since the rule results in equal resources rather than aiming at equal welfare, it avoids the burden of proof that has defeated all other proposals. We must conclude that this part of Ackerman's argument succeeds, despite the objections raised against it.[17]

Initial Equality and Individual Compensation

Not all of Ackerman's critics have focused on his justification of the principle of initial equality. Richard Flathman, for example, skirts the question of whether Ackerman's argument for initial equality succeeds:

> I leave aside the question whether this argument would go through in a world blessed with Manna; Ackerman does not have any Manna to distribute. The resources he is concerned to divide as equally as the nature of the resources allow are such goods as genetic endowments; stable families; liberal educations; freedoms to speak, assemble, associate, and reproduce; the liberty to accumulate money and other forms of property; clean, healthful environments; and so forth. In a world of finite resources, these goods compete with one another and with other goods; allocating resources to achieve, acquire or maintain one among them reduces our capacity (both individually and collectively) to achieve the others. This being the case, Ackerman's proposed allocations necessarily involve rankings of and choices among goods and hence among conceptions of good. The policies are grounded not in Neutrality among conceptions of good but in a preference for one conception of good over others.[18]

Flathman sets out an obvious objection to Ackerman's project at the level of second-best theory. Yet Ackerman has thus far been able to meet objections which, at least initially, seem quite compelling. Moreover, he claims to have anticipated this line of attack:

> although Flathman makes this point central to his critique, he explicitly

refuses to consider my theory of liberal statesmanship. Thus, he fails to discuss the way in which the liberal theory of exploitation obligates statesmen to take aggressive action against the race, sex and wealth domination that eat away at a liberal polity's dialogic legitimacy . . . Until Flathman takes such "casuistic" exercises seriously, he has not earned the right to dismiss the role of Neutrality as a constraint upon second-best policy articulation.[19]

In this section I accede to Ackerman's demand and examine his notions of exploitation and statesmanship, as he requests. I have already argued that Ackerman succeeds in justifying the basic principle of his theory, initial equality, at the level of ideal theory. Unfortunately, my examination of Ackerman's second-best theory substantiates the criticism above.

At the level of second-best theory, Ackerman seeks to justify an activist liberal state, committed to compensating those who have not enjoyed initial equality in the domains of income, education, transactional means, and genetic endowment. The key to his second-best theory is the notion of "equal sacrifice," which arises because we do not have manna and a perfect technology of justice. As Ackerman remarks: "All earthly resources would not be enough to purchase a perfect transmitter-shield or universal liberal education—let alone the entire bundle of rights encompassed by the ideal of undominated equality."[20] The principle of equal sacrifice therefore demands that each member contribute equally to the price of this imperfection. Because each person is "at least as good" as any other, none can be asked to make more than an equal sacrifice of rights to initial equality in the resources just mentioned. In other words, under actual circumstances, Ackerman's principle of initial equality becomes a principle of redress. Society is to even out handicaps so that each competes on a fair basis in the same race. Since our major concern at this point is still with the difficulties involved in taking individual claims as the subject of justice, my major criticisms are directed at the way in which Ackerman proposes to implement his principle of redress. How can he measure an equal sacrifice of rights to initial equality in a way that would tell us what each individual can claim as a matter of social justice?

As will quickly become apparent, Ackerman never systematically comes to terms with how this abstract requirement might be given concrete application. He does however, think that we can at least identify some "clear cases" of unequal sacrifice, or "exploitation." According to Ackerman, exploitation exists whenever *A* enjoys an initial advantage over *B* in at least one of his basic rights to initial equality and *B* enjoys no counterbalancing advantage over *A* in some other domain.[21] Clear cases of exploitation require only the sort of ordinal judgments Ackerman relied on in justifying the general principle of initial equality: exploitation exists as long as *A* enjoys some advantage over *B* in one domain and their respective holdings otherwise remain equal or to *A*'s advantage. For example, if we begin with two individuals of the same generation who receive equal education, transactional means and endowments, and one begins adult life with assets whose market values are greater, then the poorer citizen has been called upon to make a greater sacrifice.[22] According to Ackerman, "It should be obvious that the human race has *never* in its long history approached a moment at which a single generation's starting point was arranged in a way that approximated liberal equality. We are, in short, at generation zero."[23]

The existence of exploitation in a liberal state creates duties of "negative compensation" which requires that the initial disadvantages that *B* suffers in one area not be exacerbated further by treatment in other areas.[24] For example, those with genetic handicaps must receive an education "no less liberal" than that provided others;[25] that is, one bad turn does not deserve another. But negative compensation is not sufficient to establish the legitimacy of the liberal state. To take the same example, children with genetic handicaps must not only be given equality in other domains, but they must be *compensated* in other domains so as to approximate a situation of individual equality overall. Why do we have this further duty of affirmative action? Negative compensation by itself only perpetuates a situation of inequality—at best it keeps the effects of exploitation from expanding. But the legitimacy of a liberal state depends on wiping out exploitation, not limiting it. Otherwise we shall have a regime of unequal sacrifice, and this regime cannot be justified in a neutral way to those who have less.

At this point, the problems with Ackerman's second-best theory begin to emerge. Let us start with the relatively easy problem of negative compensation and ask how Ackerman directs us to trade off resources in education in order to compensate those who are genetically exploited by congenital blindness: "The liberality of an education is not to be measured by money spent but by insight gained, by the success with which children attain an actual sense of the domain of their freedom. Nonetheless, a point must come where the statesman must draw the line on further negative compensation and say that the (enormous) imperfections that remain in the blind child's education are no greater than those that afflict other children."[26] Somehow, we are to "draw the line." Ackerman's theory of liberal statesmanship here amounts to nothing more than an exhortation to choose wisely. Unfortunately, setting levels of negative compensation is a relatively simple problem compared with setting goals for "affirmative action." Such goals ask us to decide *how much* the blind, for example, are exploited by those who have normal vision. And, as Ackerman notes, we must again be able to put upper limits on the compensation that anyone can receive. Obviously, negative compensation and affirmative action both require much more than an ability to make ordinal judgments that tell us whether or not exploitation exists.

The necessity of developing a metric for individual claims to overall compensation arises for Ackerman in another, even more complicated way. Except for those who belong to the worst-off class or classes, everyone else has an ambiguous standing with respect to the notion of exploitation. Suppose, for example, that *A* is a healthy, poorly educated, blue-collar female living in rural isolation without easy access to transactional networks, and *B* is a handicapped, poor, fairly well educated urban male. Can we say who exploits whom and by how much? How should we weight individual claims along each dimension to arrive at an overall assessment? How should we calculate the claims of third parties with respect to redistribution between *A* and *B*? As the example indicates, nearly everyone in society can claim to be exploited, once exploitation becomes a matter of each person's overall situation, as assessed by cardinal judgments along different, weighted dimensions. Once we begin to multiply categories of relative disadvantage, we begin to generate what Rawls has called "a chaos of conflicting claims." Although I might belabor this point with additional examples, there is no need. As Ackerman himself notes, these problems, "admit only of despairing conclusions, despair no less epistemological than moral."[27]

How, then, does Ackerman propose to deal with these difficulties? His strategy at this point is to fall back on the notion of pure procedural justice. In the absence of any way of definitively settling contested issues of compensation, we are to select a particular policy by using a neutral method, for example, a lottery or a democratic voting procedure. Suppose, then, that *A* and *B* disagree about whether the best way of realizing overall initial equality is by allocating scarce resources to the poor or the ignorant. Ackerman's solution is to put such decisions to a vote. If the voting procedure (or lottery) has no built-in bias toward any particular solution, then the result is supposedly neutral with respect to any particular conception of the good. It must be remembered, of course, that neutrality is a characteristic of the procedure of selection: the result is fair because the background circumstances and rules of selection are fair, not because the result conforms to an independent standard of justice. Ackerman argues that under second-best conditions, a liberal polity will exclude from consideration all clearly exploitative policies. This will be an uncontroversial matter because we only need to make ordinal judgments about overall patterns of disadvantage in order to identify a policy as clearly exploitative.

Once all clearly exploitative policies are set aside, the second step is to find a way to select one particular set of compensating measures from the remaining class of "presumptively legitimate" policies, which are all those policies of compensation that require cardinal judgments about the relative value of competing resources. Since cardinal judgments of relative value are essentially contested, all presumptively legitimate policies are matters of "good faith disagreement."[28] Each policy has some plausibility as the best way of realizing overall initial equality, but none can be shown to be conclusively superior. Given this situation, Ackerman's solution is to design a decision procedure that is responsive to each person's recommendations but which does not favor any particular result in advance. Under third-best conditions, Ackerman builds in additional safeguards against clearly exploitative policies, for example, judicial review and a bill of rights. This, of course, makes liberal justice an imperfect procedural matter at the level of third-best, but Ackerman believes neutrality is still preserved since these constraints supposedly require only ordinal judgments.

I will not go into the details of Ackerman's argument about which particular decision procedures best guarantee procedural neutrality, for Ackerman's strategy clearly sidesteps the basic difficulty rather than resolving it. To begin with, citizens must deliberate, recommend, and justify particular policies to each other before those policies can be put to a vote. Unless the liberal state is to have no politics, in the usual sense of that word, Ackerman must still give some account of how citizens are to engage in these activities in a neutral way. How, for example, do citizens commensurate the relative value of different kinds of initial equality in trying to decide which policy best promotes overall equality? They must use *some* common metric or set of priority rules. Otherwise, the injunction to maximize *overall* initial equality is senseless, like asking us to sum together the width of this sentence and the weight of this book. Citizens cannot, however, justify any particular policy by invoking utility, the metric used for commensurating the worth of different kinds of resources, for utilitarianism clearly violates neutrality. How, then, do citizens explain their choices to each other?

The only indication that Ackerman has any common metric in mind occurs in his discussion of the size of the budget in a liberal state. He recognizes that budget expenditures reduce the resources necessary for self-regarding expenditures. Since self-regarding expenditures by individuals and public policies of compensation are both critical for self-realization, "the statesman must assess the gains in liberal value achieved by marginal increases in *B* [the budget]" against "the losses in liberal value suffered as the result of the decrease in *S* [self-regarding action]."[29] Here something called "liberal value" appears as the common metric for assessing the value of competing allocations. Clearly, some such notion is needed if Ackerman's discussion is to make sense. But what liberal value consists of is never made clear, for it is referred to only in connection with the budget and only in passing. "Self-actualization" appears to be synonymous with "liberal value" in the passage quoted above, but self-actualization is hardly a measurable attribute of general states of affairs. Expressions like "liberal value" and "self-actualization" do not make Ackerman's difficulties any more tractable; indeed, they are merely placeholders for a theory of the good that Ackerman does not provide. In any case, even if we could make some sense out of the injunction to maximize liberal value, there is a deeper difficulty. According to Ackerman's argument at the level of ideal theory, it is illegitimate to allocate resources (manna) along *any* yardstick of value, presumably even liberal value, whatever that is.

On what basis, then, can Ackerman say that all nonexploitative, controversial policies are presumptively legitimate policies? A policy is legitimate if it is neutral. But a policy does not become neutral just because it is a matter of good faith disagreement—just the opposite, one would have thought. Nor does a neutral method for selecting a nonneutral policy somehow change things. To characterize all contested policies of compensation as legitimate is a non sequitur. Ackerman never solves the problem of how to set levels of compensation in a neutral way because he does not address it. Moving questions of compensation to a procedural level only appears to resolve things.

All of this brings us back to the objection that Ackerman's proposed allocations must necessarily involve rankings of and choices among particular goods and conceptions of the good. Flathman reaches this conclusion from the premise that, in a world of scarcity, goods necessarily compete with one another. But we may make the same point in a more general way. My earlier discussion of Ackerman's justification of the principle of initial equality points to a logical difficulty that would seem to vitiate his second-best theory in advance. Ackerman's justification of initial equality succeeded precisely because it did not involve a metric for assessing the relative value of resources to individuals. Manna was assumed to be perfectly fungible, making a simple arithmetic division of all resources possible. Natural resources are hardly so flexible, as Flathman points out, and Ackerman must therefore use a yardstick of equality along some further dimension of value. But the introduction of a general metric of value departs from the initial strategy that meant Ackerman's success. On his own argument, *any* yardstick, even one that is presumptively legitimate, is nonneutral simply by virtue of measuring the value of resources along *some* dimension of value. It is therefore difficult to see how Ackerman can justify any trade-offs whatsoever without contradicting himself.

It must be remembered that this skepticism about the possibility of commensurating individual claims of redress flows from Ackerman's own position. A more reasonable view is that where society has made a set of commitments (not calculations) that provide a framework for decision, it is possible to measure the benefits and burdens of different alternatives, to make comparisons, and, where there are definite objectives and techniques, to engage in cost-benefit analysis. Ackerman's theory, however, shows that it is impossible to do these things without any definite views about the relative urgency and importance of what is to be distributed.

Once again, we cannot dismiss the general project of comparing and grading the overall claims of specific individuals just because one particular attempt to do so has failed. It is true that Ackerman's attempt to describe initial equality in resources has been no more successful than Dworkin's attempt to describe continuing equality in resources over a lifetime. Indeed, Ackerman's failure has been even more complete than Dworkin's in one respect: Dworkin does at least try to offer a metric for measuring his own version of equality, whereas Ackerman's commitment to neutrality keeps him from really offering any metric at all once we leave behind the world of manna. But just as before, when it appeared that Ackerman might succeed where Dworkin failed, it now appears that we might correct the flaw in Ackerman's account by one straightforward, albeit major, improvement in the argument. Ackerman's theory looks promising because it only involved describing a situation of initial equality, not equality over a lifetime. It therefore avoids Dworkin's problem of preserving equality over time (at least within generations). Ackerman's major difficulty, however, is that the idea of neutrality prevents him from employing a definite theory of the good, which might in turn allow him to develop a metric for assessing the overall situations of particular individuals under actual circumstances. William Galston's perfectionist theory of justice begins from a theory of the good of just this sort and so promises to overcome the major defect in Ackerman's theory. Is it possible to specify a completely fair starting point if we begin from a theory of the good such as Galston presents? To answer this question, we look at one final example of the sort of approach to social justice that Rawls believes cannot lead to workable results.

NOTES

1. Ackerman also considers the problems of third-best theory, where the full compliance assumption is dropped and we must confront the problems of free-riding, general malfeasance, and tyranny.

2. Critics have attacked Ackerman's theory in two different ways. The most important and successful criticism is that Ackerman never convincingly demonstrates why we should adopt neutrality as a basic criterion of social justice. The second line of criticism focuses on Ackerman's neutral solutions to particular problems, for example, his justification of abortion or of limited inheritance rights. I will not pursue either line of criticism, important as each undoubtedly is, because our major interest lies elsewhere, with the question of how a metric for commensurating individual claims of redress might be devised. For both sorts of criticism, see Galston, "Defending Liberalism," pp. 621-29; see also Barber, "Unconstrained Conversations," pp. 330-47; Williams, "Space Talk," pp. 367-71.

3. In another respect, however, Ackerman's principle of initial equality is not the 'starting gate' principle that Dworkin describes in Part 2 of "What Is Equality?" (nor is it clear that Dworkin has Ackerman in mind). As Dworkin points out, it would be incoherent to combine a principle of initial equality with a principle of historical entitlement if equality were thought to be the governing notion. If equal at the start, why not equal over time? Nozick's entitlement theory escapes this incoherence since it does not start with the idea of equality. But Ackerman's theory escapes this kind of problem as well, since it begins with a principle of neutrality and derives both initial equality and historical entitlement from that more basic notion. See Dworkin, "Equality of Resources," pp. 309-10.

4. Ackerman, *Social Justice in the Liberal State*, p. 4.

5. Ibid., p. 7.

6. Ibid., p. 41.

7. Ibid., p. 50.

8. Ibid., p. 54.

9. Ibid., p. 57.

10. Ibid., p. 56.

11. Ibid., p. 66.

12. Mackie, "Competitors in Conversation," p. 443.

13. Ibid.

14. Fishkin, "Can There Be a Neutral Theory of Justice?" p. 352.

15. Ibid.

16. Ackerman, *Social Justice in the Liberal State*, p. 61.

17. Since the first part of Ackerman's theory has received so much criticism,

it is worth trying to explain why his argument works in one more way. Ackerman's principle of equal shares is defensible because he assumes that there is only one, infinitely fungible resource to distribute. As I point out, this assumption allows him to postpone the the problem of comparing different kinds of resources along some additional dimension of value. If the proponent of equal fulfillment could assume that there were only one infinitely fungible kind of fulfillment, he could postpone facing this sort of problem as well. Since this counterfactual assumption is not granted to the proponent of equal fulfillment, he begins the argument at a disadvantage.

18. Flathman, "Egalitarian Blood and Skeptical Turnips," p. 361.
19. Ackerman, "What Is Neutral about Neutrality?," p. 385.
20. Ackerman, *Social Justice in the Liberal State*, p. 235
21. Ibid., p. 242.
22. Ibid., p. 240.
23. Ibid., p. 202.
24. Ibid., p. 247.
25. Ibid.
26. Ibid.
27. Ibid., p. 245.
28. Ibid., p. 273.
29. Ibid., p. 236.

CHAPTER 5

Galston and Distribution-Sensitive Consequentialism

In discussing alternatives to his own theory, Rawls identifies two variants of the principle of perfection. In the first, extreme variant, the principle of perfection is "the sole principle of a teleological theory directing society . . . to maximize the achievement of human excellence in art, science and culture."[1] In the second, moderate version, human excellence is "but one standard among several in a [pluralistic] theory."[2] In principle, both variants justify policies that have seemed intuitively unacceptable to many critics. Some of Nietzsche's writings, for example, direct us to judge society exclusively in terms of its propensity to produce great individuals. Aristotle's perfectionism is more moderate, but, like Nietzsche, his view sanctions various paternalistic practices, including slavery. Rawls acknowledges that the principle of perfection is an "attractive counterpoise" to the principle of equality when considered as one element within a "mixed" or pluralistic theory. Nevertheless, Rawls expresses a common view when he writes "to acknowledge any such principle jeopardizes individual liberty. . . . To find a firm basis for equal liberty one must reject teleological principles, both perfectionist and utilitarian."[3]

William Galston's recent perfectionist theory of justice can be understood as an attempt to retain the virtues of a teleological moral conception while avoiding the paternalistic and aggregative results that have led Rawls and others to reject consequentialism altogether. Galston's basic strategy is to revise the "maximand" of his theory so that his view becomes sensitive to distributive considerations that many teleological doctrines seem to neglect or ignore completely. He does this in three ways: (1) by presenting an objective definition of the good in terms of needs rather than preferences; (2) by including several kinds of goods in his account of human flourishing without trying to rank those goods in terms of their propensity to promote a single dominant end; and (3) by including something he calls "moral goods" in the maximand of his theory. In this chapter, I will explain the overall structure of Galston's theory by examining each of these features.

My reason for turning to Galston's theory is that it affords one final example of an attempt to devise principles for directly comparing the situations of particular individuals. In this case, however, I will criticize a theory that begins from specific principles of individual need and desert rather than from some version of equality in resources. If Galston's theory simply began and ended with these simple distributive principles it would be relatively easy to understand. The theory would direct us to balance claims of need and desert arising in specific contexts without going on to require a more inclusive estimate of each person's standing vis-à-vis every other. Unfortunately, Galston regards this sort of commonsense pluralism as "at best an elegant restatement of the problem, at worst a confession of philosophic defeat."[4] His more ambitious aim is to provide a theory for assessing "states of affairs." Because Galston takes specific individual claims as the primary subject of justice, he must assess states of affairs by their propensity to "maximize the satisfaction of valid claims."[5] This phrase requires considerable elucidation, but, briefly, Galston aims at providing principles for deciding between all of the possible ways in which individual holdings might be distributed to meet the most urgent and important needs of the greatest number of individuals.

I argue that Galston's theory fails in two respects. First, he wishes to employ personal desert as a fundamental principle of social justice. Nevertheless, he is aware of most of the general difficulties, discussed in Chapter 2, that seem to rule out personal desert as a fundamental principle, at least within the economic realm. Like Dworkin and Ackerman, Galston therefore falls back on yet another counterfactual thought-experiment in order to show how we might overcome those difficulties. Like Ackerman, Galston wishes to give everyone an initially equal start, but unlike Ackerman, Galston recognizes that we cannot even begin to define initial equality without a definite theory of the good and without an attempt to specify the sort of institutions within which economic contribution takes place. He therefore asks us to imagine a group of individuals who agree on a theory of the good, who have an equal voice in deciding how much of each resource to produce and in what way, and who then set up a perfectly just economy to award contribution on this basis. What people can legitimately expect and deserve for their contribution thus become virtually equivalent, since the entire economic system is constructed de novo to maximize everyone's potential contribution to the common good. As in previous chapters, I argue that thought-experiments of this sort are senseless. In any case, Galston's speculations are too counterfactual to serve any practical purpose, even if they could be made intelligible on their own terms.

Galston's second problem is the unworkably complex structure of the moral conception he presents. As mentioned, his theory is teleological in structure: it directs us to arrange institutions to maximize the achievement of human excellence. But as the reader may have already noticed, Galston's theory actually directs us to maximize two things: the degree to which individuals succeed in developing their potential excellence and the number of individuals whose needs for development are satisfied. As I have also mentioned, Galston develops this complicated moral structure in response to a standard objection raised against perfectionism, that is, that perfectionist doctrines permit unacceptably aggregative and paternalistic policies. Unfortunately for his objectives and aims, the adjustments that Galston must make in order to avoid these charges turn his theory into a form of pluralism rather than an alternative to it. Unlike Rawls, he offers no priority rules for systematically resolving conflicts between the various elements of his theory. This criticism of Galston sets the stage for consideration of Rawls's theory, since, by taking the basic structure as subject and by focusing on representative social positions, Rawls hopes to avoid both of the difficulties that plague pluralist theories like Galston's. According to Rawls, pure procedural justice removes the need to commensurate specific individual claims directly; and the two principles of justice and fairness are meant to provide a more comprehensive viewpoint for setting up institutions to handle the problem of conflicting first principles. I argue in the next chapter that Rawls's approach has its own special difficulties. Nevertheless, criticism of Galston helps us understand why Rawls adopts a novel view of the primary subject of justice, despite the peculiar liabilities this strategy involves.

One final note of introduction: Galston draws upon the work of a number of important contemporary moral philosophers, particularly T. M. Scanlon. In fact, his theory can be seen as a valuable attempt to work out suggestions that remain merely programmatic in the work of Scanlon and others. For this reason, as well as for the purpose of broadening my discussion, I frequently refer to these sources in trying to clarify Galston's project.

The Structure of Galston's Theory of Justice

Galston's aim is to provide a perfectionist theory of justice that can meet the sort of objections usually raised against teleological moral conceptions. He aims to do this by presenting an objective, pluralistic account of the good, and by incorporating moral goods into the maximand of his theory. Although I explain these steps in the following two sections, I am interested in the basic elements of Galston's theory only insofar as an understanding of them is necessary to elucidate the logical structure of that theory, which in turn interests me primarily because of the contrast it affords with the structure of Rawls's quite different moral conception. For this reason I leave aside questions about the details of Galston's own position whenever those questions are not directly relevant to the comparisons I wish to make.

Galston's Theory of the Good

Galston's theory of the good can most easily be understood as an attempt to develop some suggestions contained in T. M. Scanlon's influential article on "Preference and Urgency."[6] Following Scanlon, Galston distinguishes at the outset between subjective and objective theories of the good. A subjective theory of the good evaluates a person's well-being solely from the point of view of that person's preferences. An objective theory provides a basis for evaluating a person's well-being that is independent of the actual interests and desires of that person. Subjective or preference-based theories of the good have a number of attractive features. As Scanlon explains, they allow for variations in individual tastes and interests; they do not simply rank "bundles" of goods but are also "sensitive to the ways in which individuals may be affected by having those goods"; and they seem to express the equality of individuals "by giving maximum recognition to the sovereignty of individual tastes."[7] Nevertheless, Scanlon and Galston argue that subjective theories of the good are defective as a basis for assessing the equality and inequality of distributive shares. An adequate theory of justice requires an objective theory of the good.

To illustrate the defect of subjective theories of the good, consider Scanlon's example of a distributive principle that directs us to maximize equal satisfaction. Such a principle directs extra expenditures to those with special health care needs, yet this principle would also direct extra expenditures to those with trivial but expensive tastes. In general, the principle seems objectionable because it simply directs resources to the least-efficient utility consumers without requiring us to consider the importance of the preferences that are being satisfied. The problem here is not the maximizing or egalitarian character of the principle but the apparent fact that "subjective criteria of well-being seem insensitive to differences between preferences that are of great weight when these preferences are taken as the basis for moral claims."[8] Intuitively, we distinguish between preference-based claims in terms of their relative urgency, which appears to be a more basic moral notion than preference. If that is the case, then it requires explication. The purpose of an objective theory of the good is to defend some goods as more important than others regardless of the actual strength of the preferences that individuals have for those goods.

In "Preference and Urgency," Scanlon suggests two ways in which a theory of the good might explain the moral significance of relative urgency:

> I see two approaches to this problem: roughly speaking, a naturalist and a conventionalist approach. . . . [The first] would abandon the idea that the moral significance of relative urgency rests on consensus . . . and would seek to defend it as the objective truth about which interests are more important and which less so. . . . The second approach would be to defend the notion of urgency as a construct put together for the purposes of moral argument. Such a construct coincides only approximately with actual individual preferences; its usefulness stems . . . from the fact that it represents, under the circumstances, the best available standard of justification that is mutually acceptable to people whose preferences diverge.[9]

Scanlon suggests, and Rawls's later writings confirm, that Rawls's notion of primary goods provides an example of what Scanlon calls a "conventionalist" approach to the theory of the good. Rawls rejects the idea of comparing and maximizing satisfaction in questions of justice, as well as the attempt to estimate the extent to which individuals achieve their ends and the merits of those ends. Instead, he explains that "once an index of primary goods is made a part of the two principles of justice, the application of these principles with the index permits the characterization of what are citizen's appropriate claims to social resources. Although the shares that result must fit society's sense of justice on due reflection, this fit . . . *need only be close enough . . . to provide a public standard which all may accept.*"[10] Although Rawls has some scruples about the term "conventionalist," he nevertheless acknowledges that his theory of primary goods is indeed a construct put together to help us achieve agreement about which claims are relatively urgent and which are not.

Galston rejects Rawls's account of primary goods on the grounds that there are no all-purpose resources that it is rational to want whatever one's plan of life may be. In a later article, Galston argues that Rawls cannot change the explanation of primary goods so that they become means to the exercise of our two moral powers yet retain the same enumeration of those goods. It is not simply a matter of pouring old wine into new bottles:

> For example, Rawls argues that basic liberties 'allow for the development and exercise of the sense of justice'. . . . One might rather argue that the

basic liberties allow for the expression of a wide range of moral positions, many of which pull against the sense of justice. . . . In modern democracies, anyway, basic liberties seem to promote license at least as much as self-restraint—hardly a promising backdrop for the inculcation of virtues, such as justice, that demand restraint.[11]

Because Galston believes a purely instrumental account of the good is inadequate, he turns instead to the idea that there are certain invariant ends of action, as well as various instrumental goods that are rational to want in *particular* circumstances. Rejecting both utilitarian and Rawlsian conceptions of the good, Galston claims that there are four "basic" goods that must be regarded as *bonum in se:* life, the development of higher capacities, happiness, and rationality.[12] According to Galston, social justice is exclusively concerned with the distribution of these basic goods and the resources that are instrumental to their realization in specific contexts. Instrumental goods fall into four categories: economic goods (income, property, and talents), political goods (citizenship and offices), recognition goods (public honors and prestige), and opportunities for development.[13] We should note that this account of the good clearly reflects an encompassing view of the scope of social justice. Indeed, this view of the good directly or indirectly includes almost every kind of resource that it is possible to distribute.

Although a number of questions can be raised about the theory of the good that Galston proposes, most of them have no direct bearing on the theme of this book. Accordingly, I will only mention a few of the claims that he makes about the good—claims that require more explanation and defense than he has room to provide. First, Galston characterizes his list of basic goods as "basic human needs." He recognizes that, if he is to characterize his list of goods in this way, particularly the good of developing our higher capacities, he must assume that human beings are specific kinds of teleological entities. Galston admits, however, that he does not show that the concept of intrinsic teleology is "either internally coherent or compatible with the methods and results of scientific inquiry." Instead, this problem is left as an "unresolved difficulty."[14] Second, Galston claims that "we must begin by assuming that the individual deserves the basic goods that constitute the ends of need."[15] Yet he recognizes that there is no necessary entailment between the propositions that "*x* needs *y*" and the proposition that "*x* is entitled to *y*." Galston handles the connection between need and entitlement by stipulation, but, again, we require a fuller account of this relation.

Finally, Galston claims that "these principles [of the good] are widely acknowledged by those engaged in practical reasoning: to be more precise, normal judgments presuppose them and most of us can be led to acknowledge them through discussion. If these principles are subjected to a fundamental challenge, no compelling defense is available . . . the context of our belief, after some reflection, is the most powerful kind of evidence in moral argument."[16] Yet he takes Rawls to task for appealing to moral consensus in explaining the relative urgency of primary goods and in seeking to justify his two principles in reflective equilibrium. According to Galston, Rawls's appeal to moral consensus involves him in an unacceptable moral relativism. However, the passage quoted above seems to establish Galston's own theory on nothing more than a current consensus about what benefits are most important. In general, it is unclear throughout Galston's work whether our moral beliefs are self-evident or whether they rest on general agreement.[17] The metaethical basis of these views requires more clarification than Galston provides.

These unresolved aspects of Galston's account are not my present concern. Instead, I am interested in how a theory of the general sort that Galston suggests might help in meeting certain standard objections to teleological moral conceptions. One advantage has already been mentioned: an objective theory of this sort does offer an explanation of relative urgency by defending some interests as more important than others. Galston's theory of justice is not open to the charge of neglecting morally relevant distinctions between preference-based claims. As Galston notes, "many objections to utilitarianism can be traced back to the character of its maximand, subjective preferences . . . [and] these difficulties can be overcome by replacing preferences with an objective theory of the human good."[18]

The second important aspect of the theory of the good just outlined is its pluralistic character. Rather than ranking states of affairs in terms of their propensity to promote a single good, such as utility, Galston presents a heterogeneous theory of basic goods. According to Galston, the four basic goods he lists are irreducible and of equal intrinsic importance. His emphasis on the diversity of the good extends much further than this, however. In identifying the development of higher capacities as an intrinsic good, he stresses that we value many different kinds of capacities and that there is little sense in trying to rank all of the activities that best contribute to their development. In this way, Galston resists the frequent tendency of perfectionists to rank all activities in terms of a dominant end, as, for example, Aristotle seems to do at the end of the *Nicomachean Ethics*, where he subordinates practical activity to the contemplative life.[19] Galston emphasizes the diversity of human excellence because a simple rank ordering of goods obviously leads toward the subordination of many interests that we cannot convincingly treat in this way. It is implausible, for example, "to say that we value the senses, or productive activities, or the arts, or the life of the family, simply as means."[20]

As was the case concerning basic epistemological questions, Galston's treatment of higher capacities is, of necessity, brief. In fact, he only has room to list several criteria for distinguishing between higher and lower capacities. According to Galston, higher capacities are: features of our distinctive humanity, relatively rare in their fully developed forms, demanding, relatively inclusive, have a wide range of effects on others, and have been accorded wide and enduring respect.[21] Again, I will not pursue the questions that might be raised here, except to note that Galston's important emphasis on the heterogeneity of goods seems at odds with the formal maximizing or consequentialist structure of his theory of justice. As Rawls remarks about such theories, "in order to have a clear sense, a perfectionist standard must have some way of ranking different kinds of achievement and summing their values."[22] To be more precise, a pefectionist theory must have a way of summing values if it has a teleological structure. As John Finnis has demonstrated, it is also possible to develop a nonconsequentialist version of perfectionism, although Finnis's moral theory is not an account of social justice at all.[23] In the present context, however, the main point to grasp is that a pluralistic account of the good increases the number of interests that must be taken into account in maximizing excellence: in such a theory there is greater allowance for many different kinds of individuals making many different kinds of legitimate claims. A perfectionist theory of justice based on such an account will therefore have a weaker tendency toward the systematic subordination of individual interests.

Galston's Theory of Moral Goods

Even if we adopt the latitudinarian view of human excellence suggested above, perfectionism may continue to strike us as unacceptably aggregative, for even though the notion of what constitutes talent has been considerably broadened, talents themselves are still regarded as resources to be maximized. As in utilitarianism, persons are still regarded as mere locations or containers of potential or actual value. We might say that perfectionist theories take seriously the *distinctness* of persons by emphasizing differences in individual capacities. Nevertheless, they traditionally fail to take seriously the *separateness* of persons because of their exclusive concern with maximizing the good. According to Galston, this is objectionable because we regard capacities as the characteristics of specific individuals, not as resources to be moved about without reference to the individuals who possess them. As he explains, "even assuming the intrinsic worth of human capacities could be somehow quantified, it does not follow that the best policy is one that simply maximizes the sum of intrinsic worth, because this is to treat the characteristics of individuals as a disembodied unity."[24]

To avoid this result, Galston modifies the maximand of his theory in a second way. Rather than treat capacities as mere locations of potential excellence, he proposes to treat them as desert bases; and further, he proposes to incorporate moral goods directly into the maximand of his theory by counting the satisfaction of need and desert claims as *intrinsically* good, apart from the way in which their satisfaction benefits particular individuals. As Galston puts it:

> The moral goods required for an adequate view of justice are relational goods: the fitness or appropriateness of a possessive relation between a particular individual and a specific non-moral good. In moral arguments, relational goods are expressed as claims—that is, reasons purporting to establish the appropriateness of specific possessive relations. In Chapter 5, I shall argue that *need* and *desert*, suitably interpreted, constitute such reasons. Because such claims, though moral goods, include nonmoral goods as a basic element, the view of justice based on them can hope to harmonize some of the strengths of traditional nonmoral consequentialist theories with some of the deontological intuitions such consequentialism usually violates. A just state of affairs prevails, I shall say, when the satisfaction of valid claims is maximized.[25]

Scanlon makes the same suggestion, namely, "fairness and equality often figure in moral arguments as independently valuable states of affairs. So considered they differ from the ends promoted in standard utilitarian theories in that their value does not rest in their being good things *for* particular individuals: fairness and equality do not represent ways in which individuals may be *better off*. They are, rather, special morally desirable features of states of affairs or of social institutions."[26]

At this point, it will again be helpful to advert directly to another of Scanlon's recent essays, "Rights, Goals, and Fairness," in an attempt to see what Galston is trying to accomplish with the idea of moral goods. In that essay, Scanlon suggests two ways in which the notion of equality might be built into a consequentialist moral theory. The *first* way is to strengthen the notion of equal consideration which would then mean that in any justification by appeal to consequences one must give priority to those interests that are most urgent: "To neglect such interests in order to serve instead less urgent interests, even of a greater number of people, would in this interpretation, violate equality of consideration . . . [the plausibility] of such a 'lexical interpretation' is obviously dependent on the ranking we choose for determining the urgency of various interests."[27]

Galston *appears* to follow this strategy at one point by proposing a limited principle of equality:

> Considered in itself the full development of each individual is equal in moral weight to that of every other. For any individuals A and B, a policy (p-1) that leads to the full development of A and partial development of B is, *ceteris paribus*, equal in value to a policy (p-2) that fully develops B while restricting A's development to the same degree as B's was under p-1. This equivalence obtains regardless of the ways in which A's ability set differs from B's. Thus, for example, a policy that neglects the slightly retarded to the extent that they do not learn how to care for themselves and must be institutionalized is, considered in itself, as bad as one that reduces extraordinary gifts to mere normality.[28]

This principle constrains any tendency to treat capacities as a disembodied unity by making each person's all-around or inclusive claim to full development an *equal* claim, based on each person's equality qua developmental being. We may still wonder, however, exactly what such an inclusive claim to full individual development actually consists of. Unfortunately, Galston is not very clear about this, and in order to understand his principle we must again look to another theorist who seems to be trying to articulate the same idea.

A recent essay on equality by Thomas Nagel provides a relatively clear statement of the view that Galston seems to be presenting: "Each individual's claim has a complex form: it includes more or less all of his needs and interests, but in the order of relative urgency or importance. This determines both which of them is to be satisfied first and whether they are to be satisfied before or after the interests of others. An arrangement must be acceptable first from the point of view of everyone else's basic claim, then from the point of view of everyone's next most basic claim, etc."[29] It should be noted immediately, however, that the principle of equality Galston proposed is a limited or prima facie principle, because "even assuming the equal value of the full realized good of every individual . . . in practice the preservation and well-being of some individuals . . . is more conducive to the good of others," for example, "during an epidemic we should probably strive to keep doctors alive in preference to others by allocating them unequal shares of scarce food reserves."[30]

In general, Galston eschews any lexical ordering of principles, noting that the less-urgent needs of a great number may sometimes be preferred to the more-urgent needs of a few, depending on the relative urgency of need and the number of individuals involved in any particular situation. This means, however, that Galston *actually* follows Scanlon's *second* suggestion in "Rights, Good, and Fairness" about how egalitarian considerations might be built into a consequentialist theory. Scanlon suggests that different kinds of equality and fairness be regarded as independently valuable moral goods that can be traded off against other values in seeking to promote the best state of affairs overall. Or, as Galston puts it, "a just state of affairs obtains when the satisfaction of valid claims is maximized."[31]

Obviously, the structure of this theory is quite complex. Before considering its problems, it will be helpful to review the structure of the theory as it now stands. Galston begins from an objective pluralistic theory of the good that identifies basic needs for life, the development of higher capacities, happiness, and rationality. He assumes that individuals ordinarily deserve the goods that constitute the ends of need, and he also assumes that such desert creates a prima facie claim or entitlement to those goods.[32] In general, claims of need are ranked in terms of urgency and importance, with claims of desert based on contribution coming into play after claims of need have been honored. There is also a prima facie principle of equality of development that prevents any simple maximization of nonmoral goods. But particular claims of desert and need can sometimes be overridden in order to realize a greater number of less urgent claims. As we shall see, how and when this overriding takes place is not specified in any great detail. Galston begins with a commonsense understanding of justice as proportionality: greater degrees of need and desert entitle individuals to greater proportions of benefit and reward. He then tries to incorporate this commonsense understanding within a complex consequentialist structure that requires us to arrange social institutions so that these various preexisting claims of desert and need can be maximized.

In effect, Galston seems to be proposing a version of what Samuel Scheffler has recently described as "distribution sensitive consequentialism."[33] The basic idea of such a theory is that the way things are distributed within a state of affairs should itself be counted in the consequentialist calculus used to determine the best possible state of affairs overall. As Scanlon notes, such a theory differs from standard teleological theories in introducing explicitly moral goods into its maximand. These relational goods are not things that make anyone better-off; rather, they are treated as intrinsically desirable. Such a theory differs from traditional deontological views in treating different kinds of fairness and equality as moral goods rather than independent moral constraints. Equality and fairness can therefore be traded off for other values, such as efficiency. Obviously, the structure of such a theory raises many questions.

Thus far we have a consequentialist theory that says that the best overall state of affairs is one in which as many distinct individuals as possible are developing their higher capacities as fully as possible and hence are achieving their good. How to combine both maximands of a theory of this sort is, of course the central difficulty. But even before reaching this problem we must first settle on a workably noncontroversial ranking of individual needs and deserts. This presupposes that we can determine the value of different resources in terms of their relative urgency and importance, taking into account the alternative ways that any resource might be provided or substituted for. Assuming we can settle this ranking problem, on what basis do we then trade off or commensurate various kinds of fairness? How are aggregative considerations and considerations of relative urgency systematically combined, that is, when, if ever, do the less-urgent interests of many people outweigh the more-urgent interests of the few? Is it better that 99 people highly develop their capacities and only 1 fails to develop at all, or that all 100 be moderately successful?[34] It should be emphasized at once that neither Scanlon, Scheffler, nor anyone else has actually tried to give systematic solutions to the problems just raised. And although Galston claims to have done more in this respect, he is really no exception, as I argue in the next section.

Galston on Economic Justice

Now that we have pieced together the formal structure of Galston's theory of justice, it is time to look at how Galston has tried to fill in the content of this rather complex moral conception. I will take up the case of economic justice first, since this topic is central to any theory of social justice, and then consider the broader problem of balancing first principles. In general, I wish to determine two things: first, whether Galston has provided a solution to the problem of specifying an initial situation within which claims of economic desert can arise; and second, whether Galston has offered an alternative to pluralism, as he claims at the outset.

How does Galston propose we should allocate economic goods, particularly income? In general, he wishes to award income on the basis of personal desert, to define desert in terms of contribution, and to measure contribution by the satisfaction of needs. There is an important connection, then, between the measurement of need and desert: without a measure of the former we have no adequate measure of the latter. This becomes a problem for Galston because of his expansive definition of need: not only do we need a minimal set of resources to preserve the basic good of life, we also need all those resources necessary to the development of our powers and the realization of our happiness.[35] Since Galston's theory of the good permits us, in principle, to regard almost every resource as someone's potential need, we clearly require a common metric for establishing the objective value of practically every good produced. The problem of finding a common metric is just the beginning of Galston's task, however. In addition, individual development is helped or hindered by the sort of jobs people have as well as by the resources they may use. In an economy organized according to perfectionist principles, tasks must therefore be allocated in a way that somehow balances the efficient production of needed goods against the internal needs of those producing them. On top of all this, Galston notes that the very possibility of making a contribution depends on one's place in the economy and on the way in which the processes of production are set up.

As discussed in Chapter 2, a common approach to the problem of commensurating individual claims of desert is to rely on demand. I have also detailed several problems with this solution. Galston is quite aware of these problems, as is evident from his analysis of contribution. He begins by discussing at length five criteria of economic desert that are relevant within the context of a particular task. These criteria include sacrifice, the duration of work, effort, productivity, and the quality of individual products.[36] This part of Galston's analysis is relatively uncontroversial. As Rawls notes, "different conceptions of justice are likely to generate much the same common sense precepts."[37] But as I argue in Chapter 2, the principal difficulty does not arise in determining desert within smaller associations and particular economic enterprises; rather, the main problem lies in assessing economic desert *across* tasks or with reference to the entire economy considered as an ongoing collective enterprise itself. Galston recognizes this problem: "None of these [commonsense] criteria is very helpful, though, in dealing with the most fundamental problem of income distribution. What, for example, are the relative claims of the most productive doctor and most productive carpenter?"[38] He considers market demand as a possible solution to this problem but rejects it for two reasons. First, as we have stressed, Galston's theory of justice rests on an objective theory of the good, which provides a basis for the appraisal of a person's well-being that is independent of that person's tastes and preferences. The market, however, commensurates the value of resources exclusively through individual preference. Galston, therefore, cannot accept the results of allocation through a market, even a market constrained by fair background conditions, unless he assumes that all individual preferences already reflect a proper understanding of what is truly urgent and important—for what if people turn out to desire things that are not conducive to the development of their higher capacities? Galston also recognizes that measuring contribution by market-demand is circular, since such demand presupposes that we already have an initial distribution of assets. We encounter again the problem of a starting point, which Dworkin fails to solve in one way and Ackerman in another.

Given his understanding of the problems, it is surprising that at this juncture Galston falls back on a thought-experiment that emphasizes ideal demand. By comparison with the other thought-experiments we have considered, his effort is also surprisingly brief. Since his solution is so much shorter than the other speculative exercises we have discussed, we can look at it all at once:

> As a thought experiment, imagine a community of individuals, each of whom accepts, in general, the view of the human good I have advanced. They agree, that is, on the major components of the good. We then ask each of them to imagine a way of life in which his individual good has been completely achieved and to attach to each component of that realized good a weighting representing its perceived relative importance or contribution to the overall good of the individual, with the proviso that the sum of each individual's weights must be the same. For each component of the human good, the sum of the weights it receives from each individual, divided by total weights for all components, represents the relative social importance of an amount of that good that fulfills the requirements of one individual. For simplicity, let us call this amount a *unit*. We can now say that an individual's contribution is equal to the relative social importance/unit of the good he provides, multiplied by the number of units for which he is responsible. (For the number of units, see the previous discussion of average product.)
>
> On this basis we can resolve, at least in general terms, our second difficulty. The members of the community will agree that the best system of production is one that maximizes the sum of individual contributions, subject to the constraints of human and material factors of production. From this agreement, given the necessary information or assumptions, they will be able to arrive at some determination of the number of individuals who ought to be involved in the provision of each component of the good and the organization of the process of production within each sector.
>
> We arrive, then, at a general criterion of contribution: An individual's contribution is equal to the relative social importance/unit of the good he provides, multiplied by the number of units for which he is responsible, when his contribution takes place within a desirable system of

production. Later we shall discuss a proviso: The opportunity to perform tasks or functions, to make particular kinds of contributions, must be allocated on a fair and reasonable basis.[39]

I will not belabor all of the difficulties inherent in this thought-experiment, since by now most of them are quite familiar. The main problem arises in the way Galston slides from initial agreement about certain basic goods. Or very general components of individual *welfare*, to an assessment of the relative value of specific *resources*. This conceals a number of important questions, on the basis of our discussion of Dworkin: When imagining a life in which "our individual good is fully achieved," are we allowed to imagine the ownership of enormous resources as part of that life? If not, how do we take into account, in advance, the cost to others of the life we imagine leading? The thrust of Dworkin's argument is that some ideal market mechanism of discovery and adaptation is necessary to understand the effect of our choices on others and vice versa. In Galston's thought-experiment, however, each person decides which sort of life they want to lead independently of this information, and some ideal administrator (or ideal assembly?) then gathers this information together and decides on that basis what each person is to contribute. This appears to leave the determination of the value of resources dependent on whatever the contingent tastes and preferences of individuals happen to be, no matter how expensive those preferences are for others. Galston tries to overcome this difficulty by assuming that all agree on the basic elements of the good. But on the basis of our discussion of Ackerman, we know that it is not simply abstract agreement about the good that determines the value of resources for us.

Equally important is the particular structure of our life plans. Assuming that everyone agrees about Galston's list of basic goods, how are they to imagine a life in which their good is fully realized? Is it one in which they achieve their central good of personal development, no matter how ambitious? Is it a life with enough resources to enable them to constantly pursue new goals after achieving earlier ones? If no common yardstick is proposed for measuring self-actualization then there is no limit on the sort of lives that individuals can imagine as fulfilling their particular conceptions of the good. If such a yardstick is presupposed, it must be justified in a way that allows each to have an equal voice in determining the social worth of various commodities. However, this takes us back to Dworkin's notion of an initial auction, with all its attendant difficulties. But added to Dworkin's project is now the stipulation that all individuals share the same (controversial) theory of the good.

The general point is that such thought-experiments are senseless. We cannot begin with a list of basic goods and on that basis choose, from among all conceivable states of affairs, a single array of goods and services that equally reflects each person's fantasies about the particular life one would have found most worthwhile. As John Finnis observes: "There are countless aspects of happiness and self-realization, each of which may seem paramount to us at some times and not others, each of which can be participated in and promoted in an inexhaustible variety of combinations of emphasis, concentration and specialization."[40] No thought-experiment based on individual fantasies of self-fulfillment could be remotely adequate to this complexity. And even if, *per impossible*, we *could* set the initial worth of a particular array of good and services in the way Galston suggests, this would scarcely begin to address the relevant questions. According to Galston, after we determine what should be produced, we must still determine the best way of organizing production so as simultaneously to increase efficiency *and* the development of human powers *and* happiness on the job. Only after all of this is accomplished do we have a just society, that is, one in which every particular individual can make the fullest contribution possible and thereby receive what one truly deserves to receive. Galston assures us that such calculations can be carried out "given the necessary information and assumptions."[41] But, as with Dworkin's computer and Ackerman's perfect technology of justice, this assurance begs many of the important questions.

Galston himself describes the necessity of commensurating individual claims of economic desert that arise in different productive contexts as "the fundamental problem" of income distribution. It should now be clear that he fails to solve this problem. Any attempt to defend Galston must therefore drop this part of his theory and concede that individual claims within the economy must be regarded as a matter of legitimate expectations rather than as matters of personal desert in some stronger sense. These expectations are legitimate within the context of an institutional framework that is to be assessed on grounds that are more general than the relative situations of specific individuals.

With this shift in focus, we now turn from questions about precision at the level of individual claims to questions about precision at the level of first principles. Does Galston's theory provide determinate guidance at the level of first principles for assigning appropriate emphasis to the general ends of social policy? Unfortunately, Galston's theory fares no better here. By his own admission, problems of priority will emerge, since he offers a multiplicity of first principles: "*Ex hypothesis*, these problems of priority cannot be resolved by appealing to some 'higher' principle. If intuitionism (in Rawls's sense) is to be avoided, then the ordering and harmonization of principles must be based on considerations internal to the principles themselves."[42] It is unclear what it means to say that the way principles are to be balanced is internal to those principles. Galston claims that "it is entirely possible to trade-off goods that lack a common measure." As an example, he notes that "the quantity of other goods that can be validly substituted for life must be considerable."[43] But such examples do not address the relevant issue. As Rawls remarks, the pluralist does not deny that we can balance competing principles, or even that we can describe how different persons do so. A mathematical function such as an indifference curve might describe how we trade off first principles. What the pluralist denies is that there is some cogently expressible ethical conception that establishes and explains the different weights that we assign first principles when they conflict. Pluralism holds "that in our judgments of social justice we must eventually reach a plurality of first principles in regard to which we can only say that it seems to us more correct to balance them this way rather than that."[44] To say that the way we balance first principles is part of the meaning of those principles offers no guidance in this respect.

This last remark brings us back to our earlier discussion of distribution-sensitive consequentialism. If we consider this sort of consequentialism in a formal way, that is, without committing ourselves to any substantive position on how distributive and aggregative considerations are actually to be balanced, then it is at least possible that this kind of theory best expresses the structure of our judgments concerning social justice (although much more needs to be said about how fairness can be both a constraint and a good to be traded off against other goods). Perhaps we do regard particular kinds of fairness and equality as desirable in themselves but nevertheless sometimes feel justified in overriding these goals for the sake of other moral considerations. Perhaps we are willing to characterize the resulting overall state of affairs as just, "all things considered." But this is to consider only the logical structure of such a theory without specifying in substantive terms when and why aggregative considerations override considerations of relative urgency as a matter of "on-balance rightness." Our ability to agree on the substantive details, however, is precisely the issue that divides the pluralists and their more ambitious rivals.

If we consider the sort of prescriptions that Galston offers, it is clear that, on the basis of his theory, individuals can balance first principles very differently, depending on their interpretation of what is required to maximize valid claims. For example, Galston directs us to allocate developmental opportunities according to the ability of individuals to profit from them, but only where this does not preclude the production of goods that are more urgent and can be produced in greater quantity. Which opportunities and goods are these, and whose judgment of relative urgency do we rely upon? Galston tells us that harmful tasks are to be eliminated, or minimized, or shared, or compensated highly; but, again, which response is appropriate depends on the circumstances and other ends that these tasks serve. Which circumstances and ends? The economy is to be organized to maximize physical well-being, the development of our powers, and happiness, in that order. Which powers? When does an increase in the number of interests served compromise the urgency of other claims in question? Galston's prescriptions are generally unexceptionable, but they are also necessarily abstract and vague.[45] As Rawls emphasizes, "Common sense precepts are at the wrong level of generality. If all or many common sense precepts are treated as first principles, there is no gain in systematic clarity."[46]

In conclusion, it is quite important to be clear about the sort of objection that is being raised. Although Galston offers his moral conception as an alternative to pluralism, we have seen that his theory is, in fact, deeply pluralistic. To some extent, then, my objections are directed at Galston's characterization of his theory rather than at the theory itself. There is nothing inherently irrational about pluralism; indeed, social justice may be a particularly indeterminate notion, given its broad scope and complexity.

It should be noted that although Galston, in discussing economic justice, is clearly asking us to begin from a measure of each person's overall good, most of his examples outside the economic sphere deal with the allocation of a single kind of good within a fairly limited context. In my concluding chapter, I will suggest that this is generally the approach to social justice that we should take. Galston would appear to agree when he notes that goods "are divided in different categories" and that "each of these categories brings into play a distinctive ensemble of claims."[47] Unfortunately, he does not appear to be solely concerned with making certain that we distribute goods on the basis of their appropriate principles, or with keeping distinct distributive contexts from improperly influencing each other. His theory has the more positive rationale of promoting human flourishing. And although his examples usually focus on one good at a time, this underlying rationale suggests that Galston wishes to handle the problem of competing claims in other contexts in the same general way in which he deals with economic justice, namely, by choosing between different possible states of affairs in terms of their propensity to maximize self-actualization.

Finally, there is another comparison between Galston and other recent theorists that supports this interpretation. As we have seen, Scanlon suggests that we embrace a form of consequentialism that counts certain kinds of fairness and equality as goods. But Scanlon only suggests this method of justification with respect to rights, and he further emphasizes that we should justify rights by showing that they will prevent important kinds of harm rather than by showing that they maximize benefits. Scanlon insists that we must take "a fairly complex set of institutional arrangements" for granted in justifying particular rights, not because such background arrangements are necessarily desirable or "morally unimpeachable," but because they are "relatively fixed features of the environment with which we must deal."[48] In the work of Galston and theorists such as Scheffler, however, this more modest and essentially negative rationale for rights seems to be replaced by something more sweeping. It is also never very clear to what extent we must accept the background features of our society: in the economic realm we are apparently to imagine starting from scratch; elsewhere, Galston is content to begin from the needs and deserts of actual individuals.

For these reasons it is difficult to be certain about the intended scope of Galston's theory. I have interpreted Galston as offering an ambitious consequentialist theory for coordinating the allocation of goods across as well as within particular distributive contexts. It should be noted, however, that there is another interpretation of his position that brings it closer to the sort of approach I will eventually recommend.

In terms of the more general idea of a distribution-sensitive consequentialism, the failure to provide determinate guidelines is still significant. For unless the various questions that arise about this moral conception can be resolved, it remains rather empty. To date, the general moral structure that has been proposed by Galston, Scanlon, Scheffler, and others is merely a logical framework into which everyone can fit personal intuitions about how various goals might be balanced. It is less a moral theory than a way of presenting our intuitions in the guise of a theory. As the pluralist points out, it is not enough to describe how we balance first principles; rather, a systematic theory of justice must articulate an underlying moral conception that *explains* the weights we in fact assign first principles. With neither a metric for commensurating overall individual claims nor a set of priority rules, we do not have, in Rawls's terms, a *conception* of justice that can give substance to the public role that is played by the *concept* of justice. The concept of justice includes the idea of "a proper balance" between competing claims, whereas a conception of justice must give individuals some standard for resolving disputes about how the idea of "a proper balance" should be interpreted. As Rawls remarks, "If men balance first principles differently, as presumably they often do, then their conceptions of justice are different. . . . A [pluralist] conception of justice is, one might say, but half a conception."[49]

We have now reached the end of our examination of Rawls's first major claim about the sort of precision that we can expect from a theory of social justice. On the basis of the last three chapters, I think we can now safely conclude that Rawls is correct: we cannot hope to make sense of the idea of that portion of an individual's holdings that each would have "owned" in another society or in a state of nature, nor can we develop principles of justice that would somehow determine the global or overall claim that each individual can make on society. There is no way of summing all of the advantages and disadvantages that particular individuals actually enjoy, and then comparing all of these actual benefits and burdens against all of the possible benefits and burdens that the same individuals might have enjoyed in a situation of equality over a lifetime or even in a situation of initial equality. As Rawls says, this approach only generates "a chaos of conflicting claims."

Of course, it can always be replied that the arguments of the last three chapters prove nothing: we cannot infer the failure of all future attempts to devise a theory of individual justice from the failure of all past efforts. Because I am conscious of the force of this objection, I have not begun by assuming that all such theories must fail but have instead considered, on their own terms, the most sophisticated versions of this approach that are available. Dworkin's theory anticipates virtually all of the difficulties associated with preserving equality of resources over time but fails to find a solution for those problems. Ackerman's theory represents a retrenchment from equality over time to initial equality, but his commitment to neutrality precluded any way of operationalizing this more limited sort of equality under second-best conditions. Finally, Galston's thought-experiment begins with a nonneutral theory of the good but brings back all of the problems that the theories of Dworkin and Ackerman were designed to solve. Each theory can be seen as an attempt to redress the difficulties of the others, yet each reintroduces difficulties that the others try to solve. While this may not amount to proof that a metric for measuring the inclusive claims of individuals is impossible, we have canvassed all of the major alternatives, and in so doing, we have come full circle.

Alasdair MacIntyre has remarked that the idea of a proof in philosophy is usually a sterile one,[50] and eventually the plea that a certain approach is still in its infancy begins to have a rather hollow ring. If the amount of energy and intelligence that has already been invested in this approach to theorizing about social justice has not been sufficient for the task at hand, it is unlikely that further efforts will succeed. The task is a hopeless one.

As explained before, Rawls's response is to drop this approach to theorizing about social justice, shift to the basic structure as the primary subject of justice, and adopt a novel method of justification that permits certain simplifications and practical adjustments from the outset. In other words, Rawls anticipates in a general way many of the difficulties surveyed in the last three chapters and revises his approach accordingly. Of course, it is doubtful whether Rawls's own strategy can succeed, given the sort of objections it has encountered. Nevertheless, there are at least three reasons for looking at Rawls's theory once again. First, both he and his followers have revised justice as fairness in a number of ways that make it more defensible, albeit much narrower in scope. Second, many objections to justice as fairness implicitly assume that greater precision in a theory of justice is possible. But if it is impossible to arrive at a more precise account of social justice, then objections to justice as fairness that presuppose the possibility of greater precision have already missed the point. One of the aims of the last three chapters has been to avoid begging the question in this way. Third, if justice as fairness remains unpersuasive even in the light of all of Rawls's later adjustments, it seems reasonable to conclude that the relatively modest degree of precision that Rawls expects from a theory of justice is still not modest enough. For this reason, Rawls's work remains an important test case for the very possibility of devising a systematic theory of social justice.

NOTES

1. Rawls, *A Theory of Justice*, p. 325.
2. Ibid., p. 325.
3. Ibid., p. 330.
4. Galston, *Justice and the Human Good*, p. 4.
5. Ibid., p. 142.
6. Scanlon, "Preference and Urgency," pp. 655-69.
7. Ibid., p. 657.
8. Ibid., p. 659.
9. Ibid., p. 668.
10. Rawls, "Social Unity and Primary Goods," pp. 169-70 (emphasis added).
11. Galston, "Moral Personality and Liberal Theory," p. 518, n. 3.
12. Galston, *Justice and the Human Good*, p. 93.
13. Ibid., p. 193.

14. Ibid., pp. 11-12.

15. Ibid., p. 169.

16. Ibid., p. 57.

17. For an elaboration of some of the problems above, see Fullwinder's review of *Justice and the Human Good*, pp. 158-60.

18. Galston, *Justice and the Human Good*, p. 141.

19. Ibid., p. 67.

20. Ibid.

21. Ibid., p. 69.

22. Rawls, *A Theory of Justice*, p. 327.

23. See Finnis, *Natural Law and Natural Rights*, pp. 111-18, 175-76. As Finnis observes, "the inappropriate demand for precise and unqualified directives of reason in assessing responsibilities also seems to lie behind a quite different development in contemporary thought. . . . Here the feeling that it is difficult or impossible to find norms for definitively apportioning one's efforts in differing degrees amongst different potential beneficiaries seems to link up with the assumption that justice is primarily a property of states of affairs and only derivatively a property of particular decisions of ascertained persons" (p. 176).

24. Galston, *Justice and the Human Good*, p. 160.

25. Ibid., p. 142.

26. Scanlon, "Rights, Goals, and Fairness," pp. 99-100.

27. Ibid., p. 98.

28. Galston, *Justice and the Human Good*, p. 159.

29. Nagel, *Mortal Questions*, p. 117.

30. Galston, *Justice and the Human Good*, p. 162.

31. Ibid., p. 142.

32. By "entitlement," Galston means "claim" or "warrant." Nozick's notion of "entitlement" as a separate kind of moral consideration plays almost no role in Galston's theory.

33. See Scheffler, *The Rejection of Consequentialism*, pp. 26-40.

34. Ibid., p. 78.

35. Galston correctly criticizes David Miller's definition of "need" as "what is essential to a plan of life," on the grounds that this definition leaves open the possiblity of a "need-monster," that is, someone whose needs are quite excessive. But Galston's claim that we need to develop our higher faculties seems open to the same objection. Indeed, it would appear that this need can never be fully satisfied as long as our higher capacities admit of any further development.

36. Galston, *Justice and the Human Good*, p. 201.

37. Rawls, *A Theory of Justice*, p. 306.

38. Galston, *Justice and the Human Good*, p. 209.

39. Ibid., pp. 210-11.

40. Finnis, *Natural Law and Natural Rights*, p. 92.

41. Galston, *Justice and the Human Good*, p. 210.

42. Ibid., p. 58.

43. Ibid., p. 95.

44. See the discussion of intutionism in Rawls, *A Theory of Justice*, p. 38-39.

45. The problem with perfectionist theories in the present context is that they begin with lists of interests, said to be intrinsically good, which are typically drawn up in abstract terms requiring a great deal of interpretation in order to function as part of a moral theory. These lists usually differ somewhat to begin with. Galston's theory lists life, the development of higher capacities, and rationality as basic goods. But Finnis's recent perfectionist theory lists seven basic goods, including play, religion, and "practical reasonableness." The abstract nature of these theories is brought out by considering what they do not tell us: no basic good is said to stand higher than the others on these lists; none is thought to be commensurable in terms of some further characteristic; not every instance of a basic good is thought equally valuable; none is equally valuable for every person; no particular commitment to one or some combination of these goods is necessarily more rational than another for any person; finally, no rules are offered for balancing first principles of justice—rather, the way they are balanced must be "internal" to the principles themselves. See Finnis, *Natural Law and Natural Rights*, pp. 85-97.

46. Rawls, *A Theory of Justice*, p. 305.

47. Galston, *Justice and the Human Good*, p. 6.

48. Scanlon, "Rights, Goals, and Fairness," p. 104.

49. Ibid., p. 41.

50. MacIntyre, *After Virtue*, p. 241.

CHAPTER 6

Justice as Fairness

The aim of this chapter is not to pick apart Rawls's argument one more time; nor is it to try to save Rawls's argument by modifying it in various ways. Instead, I wish to understand Rawls's theory in relation to the general problem that has been my theme throughout this book. What distinguishes Rawls from other recent theorists is his sustained attention, for almost twenty years, to the question of how much precision it is reasonable to expect from a philosophical theory of justice. Rawlsian terms of art, such as "pure procedural justice," "primary goods," "representative social positions," "the basic structure," "Kantian constructivism," and "wide reflective equilibrium" all reflect that concern. Assuming that the practical problems Rawls is trying to solve are unimportant, or that a more precise account of social justice is in fact feasible, one might be tempted to dismiss his theory. But I have tried to motivate a serious reassessment of Rawls's work by showing in earlier chapters that these assumptions are unwarranted. The point of this chapter is not to argue that Rawls's theory succeeds. Even though Rawls is correct in believing that other theorists have made extravagant demands on a theory of justice, his own demands are still not modest enough. To support this conclusion, however, Rawls's theory must be reexamined carefully, both in light of the practical problems it tries to solve and by taking into account his extensive recent revisions of justice as fairness.

Up to this point I have been primarily concerned with Rawls's claim that we must take the basic structure as subject or else face unworkable complexities in trying to determine the distributive shares that each individual ought to receive. In this chapter and the next, I shift to Rawls's second general claim, namely, that we must incorporate the idea of the basic structure within a novel method of justification in order to provide an alternative to philosophical pluralism. This claim may also prove to be correct: unless we follow Rawls in permitting various simplifications and practical adjustments in the way we pose the problem of social justice from the beginning, it may be impossible to order first principles of justice in some determinate way. It is doubtful, however, whether Rawls's own theory completely achieves this aim.

Rawls takes full advantage of the permission to simplify and adjust the problem of choosing first principles. If his theory fails, even after all of the maneuvering that takes place, then it seems probable that the overall project of replacing pluralism with something more definite cannot succeed. As Rawls remarks, "It may turn out that, for us, there exists no reasonable and workable conception of justice at all. This would mean that the practical task of political philosophy is doomed to failure."[1]

In order to understand why Rawls incorporates the idea of the basic structure within a novel method of justification, it is necessary to appreciate the main difficulties that pluralism presents. As Rawls notes, there are actually several varieties of pluralism, depending on the level of abstraction at which first principles are specified. We begin with commonsense pluralism (the sort of doctrine that David Miller and Michael Walzer present). This kind of pluralism offers a family of commonsense precepts, for example, to each according to various needs, deserts, and entitlements. But, as Rawls points out, these precepts seem to be at the wrong level of generality. Various moral conceptions, utilitarianism, and justice as fairness, for example, identify much the same commonsense precepts, but weigh them differently. And, practically speaking, the way in which these precepts are ordinarily balanced is through the operation of various institutions, such as property laws, tax laws, and the market. Such institutions are in turn usually coordinated with reference to the general aims of social policy, for example, full employment, greater national product, and allocative efficiency. By this route we reach what Rawls calls a "pluralism of social ends." If we wish to explain how the general ends of social policy are to be balanced in cases of conflict, we must in turn move to an even higher level of abstraction, by identifying the first principles of what Rawls properly calls "philosophical" pluralism, for example, the principles of utility and equality. In short, Rawls contends that there is a steady pressure to make our account of social justice more abstract and comprehensive in order to a give a proper resolution to questions that initially arise in quite specific contexts. For this reason, commonsense precepts of justice seem insufficient by themselves.[2]

According to Rawls, then, it is really only at the level of philosophical pluralism that we reach the central problem facing the theorist of social justice. As Rawls remarks,

someone faced with the principles of [philosophical pluralism] may reply that he does not know what to say. He might maintain, for example, that he could not balance total utility against equality in the distribution of satisfaction. Not only are the notions here too abstract and comprehensive for him to have any confidence in his judgment, but there are enormous complications in interpreting what they mean. The aggregative-distributive dichotomy is no doubt an attractive idea, but in this instance, it does not factor the problem of social justice into small enough parts.[3]

In other words, by the time we have ascended to the level of philosophical pluralism, we encounter a dilemma. We wish a theory of justice to be sensitive to the claims of particular members of society. This we might accomplish if we were content simply to balance commonsense precepts of justice in particular situations. Yet we also want a theory of justice to be general enough to coordinate basic institutions and guide us in balancing the most general aims of social policy. Unfortunately, as our principles of justice become more and more abstract in response to the need for generality, it becomes increasingly difficult to assess the exact bearing of those principles on the situations of particular people. And, as Rawls notes, not only do our first principles become more difficult to apply, they also become more difficult to interpret or even understand. And this dilemma raises a practical question: given the apparent impossibility of meeting both demands at once, how much precision must we sacrifice, how much precision *can* we sacrifice at each level in order to reach a workable theory of justice?

The significance of Rawls's theory of justice is that it proposes to meet our requirements for precision at the levels of individual claims and first principles in a single stroke, while avoiding the problems that seem inherent at each level. Essentially, Rawls's solution is to focus on two "representative positions," that of equal citizenship and of the least-advantaged group in the distribution of social and economic benefits. By focusing on abstract social positions, rather than individuals, it is no longer necessary to follow and compare the claims of each and every individual within society. Instead, we can leave the matter of individual shares largely to pure procedural justice, as long as the least-advantaged are taken care of. The device of representative positions also enables us to deal with the problem of balancing philosophical first principles, by "factoring the problem of social justice into small enough parts." Since it is no longer necessary to try to maximize expectations with respect to more than one point of view (as we saw was the case in Galston's theory), the problem of balancing general aggregative and distributive considerations has been simplified considerably. These practical adjustments may well give us pause, but both of them seem necessary if we are to avoid the difficulties involved in trying to be fair to each and every individual and each and every social group that might possibly raise a claim on resources. The device of representative social positions seems the only solution to these problems.

Nevertheless, there are problems with this solution, as the voluminous critical literature on Rawls attests. For our purposes, however, only two kinds of objection to justice as fairness are relevant. First, it is often objected that by focusing on representative positions Rawls's theory becomes insufficiently sensitive to the fate of individuals, particularly individuals with special needs. Second, it is often objected that by focusing on the least-advantaged social position, Rawls's theory is insufficiently sensitive to the fate of all those social positions above the least well-off.

These objections are important because they seem to reopen difficulties surveyed in the last three chapters. If a theory of justice must grade and compare all of the special needs that individuals may have, then we are headed back toward the project of comparing the overall situations of every member of society. This leads to unmanageable complexities, as illustrated in Chapters 3 through 5. Similarly, if a theory of justice must balance the claims of several social positions at once, we are headed back toward pluralism. This leaves us without a definite conception of justice for the basic structure as a whole, as illustrated in my discussion of Galston. If the critics are right, Rawls's theory is unacceptable. But if Rawls's theory is unacceptable, the alternatives leave us no better off.

Of course, Rawls and his followers have tried to improve justice as fairness so that it meets these objections. For the sake of a complete discussion of the problem of appropriate precision, these improvements must be assessed. Since *A Theory of Justice* has been discussed more than enough, my discussion of Rawls's work is confined to these later revisions. I will also assume that the reader is already tolerably familiar with the "original position" and other Rawlsian terms of art.

Insensitivity to Individual Claims

Perhaps the most frequent criticism leveled at justice as fairness is that it neglects individual claims of special need. Critics usually single out health care needs, but the more general objection is that Rawls's theory does a poor job of satisfying a wide range of needs, including needs for health care, legal services, and housing. Brian Barry's objection on this score is representative:

> For Rawls a dollar is a dollar is a dollar. Whether some people need more dollars to get to the same place is irrelevant. The result of this dogma is to prevent anyone from being able to claim that because of

special handicaps he needs more income than other people to achieve the same (or less) satisfaction. Thus we rule out special allowances for the blind or otherwise handicapped. . . . *For all such individuated benefits must simply look like arbitrary inequalities if we are not allowed to look behind the distribution of income to personal circumstances which give the same income a different significance for different people.* There is no particular reason to think that most of these payments would go to those worst-off in financial terms, so the invocation of the maximin principle, however interpreted, does not get us anywhere.[4]

This sort of objection is inevitable given Rawls's emphasis on justice to groups or representative social positions. For no matter how we specify group membership, focusing on groups is bound to neglect the way in which particular members widely differ in tastes, ambitions, needs, and conceptions of the good. As Dworkin notes: "Since the members of any economic group will be diverse . . . these differences must drop away from any principle stating what true equality between groups requires, and we are left only with the requirement that they must be equal in the only dimension in which they can, as groups, possibly differ. The tie between the difference principle and the group taken as its unit of social measure is close to definitional."[5] This kind of objection is especially important because it implies that ultimately the justice of the basic structure must be assessed in terms of individual claims. Any theory that fails to take into account the special needs of individuals must be considered inadequate. The claims of particular persons, and not the basic structure, must be the basic unit of analysis for a theory of justice.

The first response to this criticism has been advanced by some of Rawls's followers rather than Rawls himself. They suggest that we revise justice as fairness so that welfare rights are built into Rawls's two principles. The general argument is that individuals in the original position have enough risk-aversion to make it plausible that they would choose to have a certain level of welfare guaranteed. As Amy Gutmann explains this strategy, welfare rights are raised to a level of priority with the first principle. This is done to secure "basic effective liberty" for all people. As Gutmann writes, "one might consider basic effective liberty a multiplicative function of formal liberties and basic welfare rights."[6] Thomas Pogge, another theorist pursuing roughly the same strategy, argues that an extensive "package" of lexically superordinate rights would be chosen in the original position, including rights to bodily and mental integrity, human interaction, access to cultural products, formal equality, the rule of law, democratic self-determination, liberties of thought, conscience, speech, and association, equal attention in education, and a right to medical treatment equivalent to that available to others with similar ailments.[7] The strategy of Pogge and Gutmann capitalizes on the fact that Rawls's theory identifies two distinct sorts of "representative social positions." Besides the position defined by a person's place in the distribution of income and wealth, there is also the representative position of equal citizenship. In effect, the revisionists suggest that rights of citizenship be greatly expanded in order to accommodate the objection from special needs.

At first glance, Rawls's most recent writings would seem to endorse this strategy. In the 1982 Tanner Lectures, for example, Rawls says that we should try to find a list of basic liberties which, when made part of the two principles of justice, leads the parties to agree to justice as fairness. This achieves the "initial aim" of justice as fairness "by showing that the two principles provide a better understanding of freedom and equality in a democratic society than the first principles associated with the traditional doctrines of utilitarianism, perfectionism or [pluralism]."[8] Rawls then suggests that we try to find a second list of liberties such that the parties would agree to the two principles with that list rather than the initial one. In principle, there seems to be no reason why we cannot go through an extremely detailed indefinite series of such improvements until we emerge with an extremely detailed list of liberties and rights.

It should be noted, in passing, that in the Tanner Lectures a great deal of argument now takes place before we reach the original position. Rawls draws on our own history of constitutional interpretation to explain the arrangement of basic civil and political liberties in one system. This system or list is then presented to the parties in the original position on an all or nothing basis. Unfortunately, this raises the possibility that we will never actually reach the argument from the original position, for controversy over the list of basic liberties itself may supervene. I will leave this problem for my final chapter, however, for even if the system of equal liberties that Rawls presents is acceptable, there is still a serious difficulty in extending that list to cover welfare rights. Rawls himself points out this difficulty a little later on in the Tanner Lectures: "Whenever we enlarge the list of basic liberties we risk weakening the protection of the most essential ones *and recreating within the scheme of liberties the indeterminate and unguided balancing problems we had hoped to avoid by a suitably circumscribed notion of priority.*"[9]

This problem is as crucial as it is obvious, yet the revisionists inexplicably pass over it. After compiling his extensive package of basic rights, Pogge says, parenthetically, "throughout, I do not deal with the question of how to balance these rights in cases of conflict."[10] Gutmann is equally elusive. She claims that, "The distribution of medical and legal services according to need would be a more rational decision from the perspective of the original position" but adds, in a footnote, "This is of course not to say that needs even in the cases of medical and legal care can be determined simply."[11] She also notes that her revised egalitarian first principle "clearly requires additional specification. The precise nature of the function constituting basic effective liberty must be further specified. Plausible limiting conditions are also necessary to avoid the problem of resource drainage that extreme cases present, but these conditions can only be determined once the contours of need and income distribution are known in any given society. We leave open here what the process or nature of this specification may be."[12]

To put it bluntly, it is doubtful whether individuals behind the full veil of ignorance have enough information to be able to settle on specific levels of welfare and to determine in advance how they will balance conflicting need-based claims on resources. As Rawls says, "the discriminating power of philosophical reflection at the level of the original position may soon run out."[13]

The second basic difficulty with this revisionist strategy is that even though a process of revising the list of basic liberties is generally endorsed by Rawls, this process cannot be taken very far without losing sight of his essential rationale for focusing on the basic structure in the first place. That rationale is to make a theory of social justice a manageable enterprise by confining it to the task of selecting principles of appropriate generality. For this reason, it does not seem consonant with Rawls's general approach to argue that his theory requires a specific set of welfare rights for different basic structures. The policies that a particular society governed by the two principles will choose for guaranteeing a satisfactory minimum depend on information available only at later stages of Rawls's four-stage sequence. As Tom Beauchamp observes, "alternative proposals regarding rights to health care, no federal or state funding of health care, or some combination of private and public provision probably all have versions consistent with Rawls's theory (contingent on the particular facts)."[14] Nor is there any reason to assume that a health care system must be an institution within the basic structure. For under some circumstances access to health care might be handled on a free market basis.[15] As Rawls notes, it is often unclear which of several economic and social arrangements would be chosen, even at the legislative stage of his four-stage sequence. "But when this is so, justice is to that extent also indeterminate. Institutions within the permitted range are just, meaning that they could be chosen. . . . Thus on many questions of social and economic policy we fall back on a notion of quasi-pure procedural justice: laws and policies are just provided they fall within the allowed range. This indeterminacy is not itself a defect. It is what we should expect."[16]

For the above reasons, Rawls's own defense against the charge of unfairness to individuals is somewhat different. Instead of arguing that individuals might choose a specific package of welfare rights in the original position, Rawls instead suggests that we leave detailed specification of the two principles to the later stages of his theory. As the veil of ignorance is progressively lifted for the purpose of making constitutional and legislative decisions, the parties fill in the more specific set of institutions and rights suitable to their own circumstances. The above considerations also explain why Rawls begins by assuming that all citizens of a well-ordered society have physical and psychological capacities within a normal range. He does so because, "the first problem of justice concerns the relations between citizens who are normally active and fully cooperating members of society over a complete life."[17] Finally, once the problem of normal medical needs (and other services) has been settled, it may prove possible to bring the problem of special needs back into the picture: "The weights for the index of primary goods need not be established in the original position once and for all, and in detail, for every well-ordered society. What is to be established initially is the general form of the index and such constraints as that expressed by the priority of the basic liberties. Further details for practice can be filled in progressively in the later stages as more information becomes necessary."[18]

There are several points to be made about this solution to the problem of unfairness to individuals. First, comparing this solution with Ackerman's proposal, discussed in Chapter 4, we can see a superficial similarity between the two which only underscores an essential difference. Recall that Ackerman felt that the problem of compensating particular individuals led to despairing conclusions, "despair no less epistemological than moral." In the face of the difficulty of making interpersonal comparisons, Ackerman's solution would leave all "contested cases" of compensation to the legislature of a liberal society. The difficulty with this solution, however, was that it seemed inconsistent with his insistence that a liberal state be neutral with respect to all conceptions of the good.

Justice as fairness does not suffer from this difficulty. In "Fairness to Goodness" Rawls notes that, "the original position is as a whole not neutral between conceptions of the good in the sense that the principles of justice permit them all equally. Any definite agreement is bound to favor some conceptions over others."[19] But further, Rawls now emphasizes that the constraints of the original position presuppose a particular "non-neutral" conception of the person. In theory the purpose of setting up constraints on later decision-making procedures and then allowing a procedural solution is not, as in Ackerman, to protect neutrality. Rather, these later constraints also express the idea that in a well-ordered society, citizens are regarded as free and equal. Rawls's proposal to delay the handling of special needs until the legislative stage does not involve a non sequitur as did Ackerman's attempt to commensurate different kinds of resources without providing a theory of the good. There is no inconsistency in Rawls's argument that we should leave certain problems to the legislative stage when they prove beyond philosophical resolution. As long as these legislative decisions are suitably constrained, the aim of justice as fairness is preserved.

The second point about Rawls's strategy for dealing with special needs has to do with the difficulty of this problem. As Daniels points out, any objection to Rawls's theory based on its inability to handle the problem of special needs appears less damaging when we reflect on the fact that no theory of justice has dealt adequately with this problem.[20] For example, if we adopt the view that justice always requires us to give the urgent needs of particular individuals complete priority (a view that seems implicit in the opening quote from Barry), one faces Charles Fried's objection that this opens up a "bottomless pit" of expenditures on health care. In addition, any view that focuses on particular needs must define the notion of need across a wide range of cases, so that it covers, for example, various "mental-health" needs as well as physical needs. This definition must be relatively uncontroversial and must permit us to construct a ranking of different kinds of need in some order of priority. I reviewed some of the problems facing such a definition in discussing Galston's theory.

Finally, the strategy of meeting special needs through an insurance market, suggested by Fried, Dworkin, and others, does have the apparent merit of putting upper bounds on compensation. But, as Daniels notes, this approach is intuitively acceptable only if it allows persons to buy a "reasonable" amount of health care, and this seems to take us back to the idea that shares are fair only if they meet special needs.[21] Yet the idea of a market is to define fair shares independently of needs, so that once individuals have been given fair shares they can determine what counts as "need" through their preferences. Thus, this approach seems to leave the determination of what counts as need to the market in a way that may prove unacceptable.[22] In view of these difficulties, there is some justification for initially limiting inquiry to the problem of justice as it arises between individuals with mental and physical capacities that fall within a normal range.

Notwithstanding the difficulty of the problem, however, it seems clear that Rawls's solution is unsatisfactory. There is not enough information in the original position for individuals to agree on some definite set of welfare rights. And if the parties instead agree to "the general form" of an index for primary goods, leaving the details for later on, how do they know what they are agreeing to, or whether it will even be possible to agree once more information is provided? There might be some motivation to follow Rawls in waiving the problem of special needs, if he could at least provide a solution to the more basic problem of indexing for normal, healthy individuals. But in fact no such solution has been forthcoming. In trying to identify the "least well-off" through an index of primary goods, Rawls is committed to providing a measurement of relative disadvantage that commensurates all of the following goods: the powers and prerogatives of offices and positions of responsibility in all of the main economic and political institutions of the basic structure, income and wealth, and the social bases of self-respect. Leaving aside the numerous problems in identifying and measuring each of these goods, there remains the problem of assigning a relative weight to each part of the index.[23] This is not simply a small, technical aspect of the problem of social justice; in some respects it is *the* problem.

Although Rawls fails to address the indexing problem at any length (much less solve it), it is nevertheless crucial to note that the problem itself represents a much simpler version of what other recent theorists have tried to do, for the problem of commensurating different resources is now at least defined relative to a single social position rather than relative to every member of society at once. Most theorists of social justice begin where Rawls leaves off, but it appears that in many respects this is a step backwards. Once the problem of evaluating the overall standing of even *one* position proves too hard, it hardly seems sensible to multiply difficulties by trying to do as much for *all* social positions.

Of course, if we give up the project of constructing an index, we may also have to surrender the idea that "the basic structure" is the primary subject of justice. It becomes increasingly difficult to regard basic institutions, *organized as a whole,* as our primary concern. For without a comprehensive measure of the overall standing of even one position, we have no single reference point by which to coordinate those institutions. I shall return to this difficulty at the end of this chapter. For the moment, it is enough to point out that Rawls's failure to solve the indexing problem has wider implications for his theory than is generally realized.

Insensitivity to Group Claims

The General Problem

The second objection to justice as fairness that concerns us is the charge that Rawls's "difference principle" neglects the expectations of all social positions above the least well-off. It supposedly does so by requiring policies that are of minimal benefit to the least advantaged, yet quite harmful to those in higher positions; and by forbidding policies that are mildly harmful to the least advantaged, yet greatly beneficial to those above. To put it another way, the difference principle appears insensitive to changes in aggregate welfare. This problem is obvious. As Rawls himself remarks, "it seems extraordinary that the justice of increasing the expectations of the better placed by a billion dollars, say, should turn on whether the prospects of the least favored increase or decrease by a penny."[24] What is less obvious, but of central relevance to the concern of the book, is that this objection to the difference principle is only one instance of a quite general difficulty that seems to face *all* principles of justice for the basic structure.

In order to explain this general difficulty, it will be helpful to recall Rawls's rationale for focusing on the basic structure in the first place. By taking representative social positions as the subject of a theory of justice, "it is no longer necessary . . . to keep track of the endless variety of circumstances and changing relative positions of particular persons. One avoids the problem of defining principles to cope with the enormous complexities which would arise if such details were relevant."[25] By the same token, however, this radical simplification of the problem of justice means that principles for the basic structure can really only take into account two things: positions and pay-offs, or shares of value. In other words, principles for the basic structure must be what contemporary theorists call "end-state" principles. As Nozick explains, "People in the original position either directly agree to end-state distributions, or they agree to a principle; if they agree to a principle they do so solely on the basis of considerations about end-state distributions. The *fundamental* principles they agree to, the ones they can all converge on agreeing upon, *must* be end-state principles."[26] Once we understand that all principles for the basic structure must be end-state principles, the general difficulty begins to emerge. For it turns out that apparently *no* end-state principle can be at once suitably neat and clear, thereby providing an alternative to pluralism, and, at the same time, intuitively satisfactory.

This point has been nicely demonstrated by Douglas Rae, who has shown that all end-state principles violate what Rae calls a principle of "simple justice."[27] Rae's principle of simple justice states that we should never accept any arrangement that distributes less (in total) less equally. Using Rae's example, we can illustrate how Rawls's difference principle apparently violates this rule. Consider a choice between two possible allocations, X and Y:

POPULATION	X	Y
Top 5%	31	100
Middle 90%	30	20
Bottom 5%	10	11

As Rae explains, the difference principle would apparently require us to choose Y. But Y has a lower average benefit and distributes shares less evenly. In other words, the difference principle asks us to distribute less in total, less equally.[28] This problem is not peculiar to the difference principle, however. Using such examples, Rae shows that principles of utility and equality, as well as the difference principle, violate his simple rule of justice. As James Fishkin explains: "any aggregative principle (such as the principle of utility) is necessarily insensitive to distributive objections that must, at some point, if they are great enough, become overwhelming; and any distributive principle (such as maximin or equality) is necessarily insensitive to aggregative objections that must also, at some point, if they are great enough, become decisive."[29] To summarize: all principles for the basic structure must be end-state principles, which are neat and clear, so they provide an alternative to pluralism. But all end-state principles lead to outcomes we cannot accept.

The problem is even more serious, however, since Rae has also shown that there seems to be no way of specifying an acceptable hybrid principle which does not violate the requirement of transitivity. Rae specifies his hybrid principle with two rules: (1) choose any allocation that favors some without disadvantaging others; (2) if no alternative favors this "general advantage," choose the more equal allocation. As Rae and Fishkin point out, the basic difficulty is that this principle of "simple justice" uses alternating aggregative and distributive clauses. This means that we can prefer allocation B to A on aggregative grounds, C to B on distributive grounds, and C to A on aggregative grounds again, thereby setting up a vicious circle.[30]

On the face of it, there seems to be no reason why a hybrid principle should be set up to use alternating clauses in this way. But a moment's reflection will indicate the difficulty with any alternative approach. A more adequate principle that would satisfy transitivity conditions would have to select between states of affairs by ranking alternative *combinations* of equality and utility. But this simply reintroduces the problem of balancing these general considerations, without providing any principled grounds for saying why we should prefer one combination over another. By a slightly different route, we have come back to the idea of a distribution-sensitive consequentialism discussed in the last chapter. And once again it is difficult to regard this kind of theory as an alternative to pluralism. For how are we to balance total or average utility against equality in the distribution of satisfaction? As Rawls observes in the passage quoted above, "not only are the notions involved here too abstract and comprehensive . . . but there are enormous difficulties in interpreting what they mean."[31] Of course, I have already discussed some of those difficulties in Chapter 5.

The argument of Rae and Fishkin, then, amounts to a sort of impossibility theorem, and the alternative presented by Galston, Scheffler, Scanlon, and others is not a real alternative. If Rawls cannot find a response to this argument, we must conclude that there is very little hope of replacing pluralism with something more systematic. Powerful as this argument is, however, it has an obvious weakness. Rae and Fishkin present us with lists of payoffs to positions without explaining how these lists arise, or even whether they could arise under any circumstances we are likely to encounter. In other words, they treat social justice as a matter of "so many abstract possibilities." Under what circumstances, for example, would we actually be called upon to sacrifice a billion dollars for a penny? Obviously, we will *never* be able to devise a determinate theory if we must show that end-state principles lead to satisfactory results in all possible worlds. But according to Rawls, this is precisely the demand that Fishkin and Rae make. As Rawls observes,

> the problem of social justice is not that of allocating *ad libitum* various amounts of something among given individuals. Nor is there some substance of which expectations are made that can be shuffled from one representative man to another . . . the possibilities which the objection raises cannot arise in real cases. . . . We should note that the difference principle not only assumes the operation of other principles but it presupposes as well a certain theory of social institutions.[32]

For our purposes this response is important, not because it succeeds, but because it is the only response that could possibly succeed. Unless a theory of justice can rely on various empirical assumptions about how just institutions are likely to work in practice, we are stuck with the dilemma just outlined. The function of these empirical assumptions is to define what Rawls calls the "feasible set" of outcomes that can be produced by a well-ordered society organized according to justice as fairness. By defining the feasible set in this way, it is hoped that objections of the sort made by Rae and Fishkin are ruled out. Rawls's theory of institutions is therefore an integral part of his overall argument. In fact, it is now the key part of his revised argument for the difference principle, as I show below.

The Revised Argument from the Original Position

Although Rawls has recently modified justice as fairness in a number of ways, he has not yet tried to piece all of those revisions together to show how the problem of rational choice in the original position has changed. Before we can assess his argument, then, we must complete this task. I will not give a full account of Rawls's revisions, however, or try to defend them here. My purpose is only to show that every part of his contractarian argument except his theory of institutions now depends on extra-contractarian assumptions about moral personality. I believe Rawls's new emphasis on the idea of moral personality makes his revised theory more coherent, albeit much narrower in scope. But as I have indicated before, a discussion of different conceptions of the person lies outside the scope of this book. In contrast, Rawls's theory of institutions is central to the question of appropriate precision.

In *A Theory of Justice*, Rawls argued that the parties in the original position would choose his two principles because they "maximize the minimum" share of primary goods that might be expected once the "veil of ignorance" is lifted. In order for a "maximin" rule of choice to be rational, however, a bargaining situation has to satisfy the following conditions: (1) Since the rule takes no account of the likelihood of possible circumstances, there must be some reason for sharply discounting estimates of probability; (2) The rejected alternatives must have outcomes that one could hardly accept; and (3) The person choosing must have a conception of the good such that he cares very little, if anything, for what he might gain above the minimum stipend. Rawls initially argued that various features of the the choice behind the veil of ignorance satisfied these conditions "to the highest degree, taking them to the limit, so to speak."[33] His early critics, however, could find none of these features exemplified in original position. In response, Rawls has changed his explanation of the way that each of these features is represented in the initial bargaining situation.

The first revision to justice as fairness that we must consider is perhaps Rawls's most important, philosophically speaking. I consider it first, however, in order to put it to one side: with respect to the problem of rational choice in the original position, this revision turns out to be relatively insignificant. Originally, Rawls's theory was set up to provide a neutral framework for deciding between several traditional alternative conceptions of justice. That aim has now been abandoned. In "Social Unity and Primary Goods," Rawls now stipulates that he is only seeking a conception of justice for a "liberal" society. According to Rawls, the underlying philosophical presupposition of liberalism is that citizens embrace a plurality of final ends which are not only in conflict but incommensurable.[34] Obviously, this stipulation rules out almost all of the major alternatives to justice as fairness from the beginning, particularly utilitarianism, since that doctrine presupposes the sort of interpersonal comparisons now deemed inappropriate in a liberal society. This is not to say that utilitarianism is false. Rather, it is to insist that the assumption that there exists a utility function that matches all citizens's judgments in making interpersonal comparisons of welfare is at odds with the conception of moral personality presupposed by a liberal order. The idea of a shared "highest order preference" or utility function seems to neglect the distinctiveness of persons, by supposing that individuals are ready to change their characters and final aims in pursuit of greater well-being, as defined by some public ranking. It also neglects the notion of autonomy, by regarding individuals as equal primarily in their capacity for satisfaction rather than in their capacity to form, revise, and pursue a conception of the good.[35] As Rawls remarks, in utilitarianism it seems as if "Neither persons nor associations have arrived at or fashioned a conception of the good and of how to lead a life which is peculiarly theirs."[36] For this reason, a liberal society must find a basis for assessing claims of justice that is more in accordance with our understanding of persons as free and equal. That is what Rawls's revised account of primary goods is meant to accomplish.

Rawls's various attempts to show that utilitarianism is incompatible with the philosophical presuppositions of liberalism may well be the core of justice as fairness. In the present context, however, it is not necessary to evaluate those attempts. The question that must be settled here is quite a bit simpler: how does his extra-contractarian argument against the utilitarian understanding of the person and of social unity affect the problem of rational choice in the original position? In one sense, not very much. It is a philosophical mistake to think that justice as fairness can be transformed into an a version of utilitarianism by the formal maneuver of redescribing preferences for primary goods in terms of utility functions for those goods. As Rawls points out, "the problem of interpersonal comparison in questions of justice goes to the foundations of a conception of justice and depends on the conception of the person and the way in which social unity is conceived."[37] But granting this point, the parties in the original position still wish to do as well for themselves as they can in terms of their respective share of primary goods. All that Rawls has done, therefore, is to replace the possibility that the parties might choose to maximize average utility with the possibility that they might choose to maximize the average share of primary goods. Rawls has changed the value numeraire for the calculation of rational advantage in the original position, but he has not thereby given any reason why the parties would choose maximin over a principle that directs society to maximize the average.

Having put Rawls's arguments against utilitarianism to one side, we are now ready to consider the other revisions that might affect the problem of choice in the original position. The first question, of course, is whether Rawls has given any new reason why the parties in the original position might discount probabilities. It will be remembered that one of the reasons he thinks that the parties would adopt his two principles in the original position is that they do not have the information that would allow them to estimate their probability of occupying various class positions once the veil of ignorance is lifted. In the absence of such information, the safe course is to adopt principles which maximize the minimum share they might receive.

Of course, Rawls did give another reason for adopting such a conservative strategy, namely, that the decision will determine one's life prospects and therefore is too important to gamble on. This consideration would provide strong grounds for discounting some probabilities even if we had knowledge of them. But as many critics have pointed out, this only applies with regard to the worst outcomes. The question is why Rawls also excludes knowledge of probabilities for all those distributions above an acceptable minimum. Why does the veil of ignorance exclude knowledge of the number of persons in each social position, as well as knowledge of which social position each person will occupy once the veil of ignorance is lifted? Rawls's original rationale was that it is impermissible to sum advantages and disadvantages over persons. But as Nagel and others have remarked, this is supposed to be one of the conclusions of the contract approach, not one of its presuppositions.[38] In any case, knowledge of probabilities does not impeach the impartiality of the choice situation. As long as individuals do not know their own particular fates, impartiality between persons is preserved.

Rawls has implicitly recognized the force of this criticism, by now arguing for "the thickest possible veil of ignorance" on the grounds that "the parties are not to be influenced by any particular information that is not part of their representation as free and equal moral persons."[39] Like everything else in his revised account, the exclusion of an objective basis for probabilistic calculations is now explained by a certain conception of the person, not by the demands of impartiality alone. At the same time, however, while the parties do not have enough information to gamble on the likelihood of occupying a particular social position, they do know that they are choosing principles under "reasonably favorable conditions." These conditions "are determined by a society's culture, its traditions and acquired skills in running institutions, its level of economic advance (which need not be especially high) and no doubt by other things as well. I assume, as sufficiently evident for our purposes, that in our country today reasonably favorable conditions do obtain."[40] This adjustment reflects the idea that we are now trying to settle the just form of basic institutions "within a democratic society under modern conditions" rather than trying to devise a universal theory of justice.

These two assumptions do not conflict: the stipulation that social cooperation takes place under "reasonably favorable conditions" does not require that those conditions be spelled out. It is much less specific than the information necessary to calculate social positions, and is therefore compatible with the idea of a "thicker" veil of ignorance. However, the knowledge that social conditions are "reasonably favorable" also means that the alternatives to Rawls's two principles are no longer as likely to have "outcomes that we could hardly accept." We therefore have to consider Rawls's new explanation of how the choice in the original position exemplifies this second feature leading to maximin.

I will be quite brief about Rawls's new explanation of this aspect of the choice in the original position. In the Tanner Lectures, he argues that the priority of liberty is necessary to secure effective conditions for the exercise of the two moral powers attributed to members of a well-ordered society. This argument makes the suppression of liberty an "intolerable" outcome almost by definition. For example, in discussing the grounds for liberty of conscience Rawls remarks: "If someone denies that liberty of conscience is a basic liberty and maintains that all human interests are commensurable, and that between any two there always exists some rate of exchange in terms of which it is rational to balance the protection of one against the protection of the other, then we have reached an impasse."[41] Although he notes that this passage does not, strictly speaking, amount to an argument, he also says that it expresses the fundamental ground for the priority given to liberty of conscience. I will not try to summarize the arguments for the other basic liberties here. For present purposes, I will assume that, given the way in which the original position is now modeled on a certain conception of the person, the priority of a system of equal basic liberties is both necessary and assured.

Finally, let us consider the third feature of the original position leading to maximin, namely, the idea that the parties have conceptions of the good such that "they care little if anything about what they might receive above the minimum." For a number of reasons, this is clearly an implausible assumption to attribute to the parties in the original position. To begin with, they simply do not have enough information about their own life plans to judge whether they will be completely satisfied by the minimum stipend. But as Steven Strasnick noted long ago, Rawls needlessly overstated his argument when he said that the original position exhibited each of the features leading to maximin "to the highest possible degree."[42] Since all of these features are intended to work together, Rawls's argument will still be strong even if each one is weakened somewhat, and he has modified his explanation of this third feature. In "Social Unity and Primary Goods," he attributes a capacity to take "responsibility for ends" to members of a well-ordered society as part of their notion of moral personality. Although citizens in a well-ordered society may in fact turn out to care for more than the minimum stipend they receive, this capacity insures that they are nevertheless "able to moderate the claims they make on their social institutions in accordance with the use of primary goods. Citizens' claims to liberties, opportunities and all-purpose means are made secure from the unreasonable demands of others."[43]

According to Strasnick, once we weaken the third condition leading to maximin, the actual nature of Rawls's argument begins to emerge: "For Rawls apparently does not intend to argue that the parties in the bargaining game care little if anything for what they might achieve above a minimum. . . . Rather, he will argue in later sections and especially in Part II of *A Theory of Justice* that since 'these principles provide a workable theory of justice, and are compatible with reasonable demands of efficiency . . . this conception guarantees a satisfactory minimum.' "[44]

This argument, together with the idea that the alternatives are unacceptable, then seems to lead to Rawls's conclusion. For given that the two principles guarantee a minimum that is not just tolerable but satisfactory, and that the alternatives might put one below the minimum in a way that is unacceptable, that is, allow the suppression of basic liberties, there appears to be no reason for the parties to try to do better. If this is indeed the nature of Rawls's argument, then, as Strasnick concludes: "Obviously, the ultimate success of this argument will depend on whether Rawls can establish that the application of his principles will lead to a 'satisfactory' and workable conception of justice."[45]

If Rawls is to reconstruct the argument from the original position in light of all the criticisms that his earlier version faced, this is the form that such a reconstruction must take. Rawls must stipulate that the parties do not have enough information to make probabilistic calculations; assure the priority of liberty; weaken the assumption that the parties care nothing for what they might receive above a minimum; and, finally, use the theory of institutions in Part II of *A Theory of Justice* to show that the two principles are "satisfactory" and "compatible with reasonable demands of efficiency." Note what has happened to the problem of choice in the original position given all of the revisions above. Utilitarianism has been ruled out. The priority of liberty appears to be guaranteed. And, of course, given the great importance of the decision in the original position, the parties will choose a conception of justice that guarantees them a minimum economic stipend, regardless of whether they can calculate probabilities or not. In short, the choice in the original position has silently dwindled to only two alternatives: either Rawls's two principles, or what he calls a "mixed" conception of justice. "Mixed" or pluralistic conceptions of justice also recognize the priority of liberty. They differ from Rawls's two principles only in directing society to maximize the average share of primary goods once a suitable minimum has been determined by intuition. The *only* question that now remains for the parties in the original position is whether there is any reason for preferring Rawls's two principles over this alternative.

At this stage, the reader may be tempted to dismiss this last remaining choice as trivial. But if we try for a moment to think about the problem that Rawls is posing in a less abstract manner, we will see that he is still addressing one of the central problems facing the modern, liberal welfare state. In our own society, for example, the priority of a system of equal basic liberties is a relatively settled notion, although there is still controversy over how those liberties are to be regulated within that system. In contrast, we are much more divided on the question of whether we should replace the idea of "careers open to talents" with what Rawls calls "fair" equal opportunity. "Fair" equal opportunity asks us to redress natural as well as social contingencies and therefore requires something like the difference principle. The choice in the revised original position is also significant because one of the central aims of justice as fairness is to offer an alternative to our current practice of setting a welfare floor by intuition. Whether the parties can choose between these two alternatives, then, will presumably determine whether Rawls has succeeded in settling the most controversial aspect of social justice in a liberal society, namely, the way in which basic social and economic inequalities ought to be arranged.

It should also be more apparent now why Rawls's theory of institutions has become the crux of the contractarian part of his argument. For it is the only part of his original theory that is not now explained in terms of extra-contractarian assumptions about the nature of moral personality and social cooperation. Of course, we may reject those assumptions in favor of another starting point. But this rejection would not by itself show that Rawls has failed to work out at least one coherent interpretation of social justice in a modern, liberal democratic society. On the other hand, if Rawls's theory of institutions does not perform its proper function in the revised argument from the original position, Rawls's account of justice fails on its own terms. It will no longer be necessary to consider whether there is another ideal of moral personality that is well defined and general enough to serve as the basis of a theory of justice for the basic structure. The first order of business, then, is to examine Rawls's claim that institutions organized according to his two principles will be workable and guarantee a satisfactory minimum.

Rawls's View of Appropriate Precision in a Theory of Justice

Offhand, it would seem rather easy to reject Rawls's claim that his two principles will provide a satisfactory minimum. This claim is quite vague. But of course the same objection can be made to the choice of a mixed conception of justice in the original position as well: how do the parties know that choosing to set a welfare floor by intuition will prove satisfactory? This common difficulty seems to show that the choice posed in the original position is indeterminate. Indeed, it suggests that we should abandon the contractarian part of Rawls's argument altogether, since we apparently cannot begin to determine what will count as a satisfactory minimum without considerably more information than even the revised original position allows. Rawls is aware of this objection, however. In response, he takes us back to the problem from which we began, namely, the inadequacy of our ordinary practice of balancing first principles by direct appeal to our considered judgments.

In arguing against mixed or pluralistic conceptions of justice, Rawls clearly anticipates the kind of difficulties raised by Fishkin and Rae. In fact, his notion of a mixed conception of justice and Rae's later principle of simple justice are identical. As Rawls remarks, the problem with a mixed conception of justice is that it only tells us that, "provided a certain floor is maintained, greater average well-being and a more equal distribution are both desirable ends. . . . The fact is, we do not in general agree to very much when we acknowledge ends of this kind. . . . One is in effect being told to exercise one's judgment as best one can within the framework of these ends. Only policies preferable on each score are clearly desirable."[46] But as Rawls goes on to say:

> Anyone using the two principles of justice might also appear to be striking a balance between maximizing average utility and maintaining an appropriate social minimum. If we attend only to his considered judgments, and not to his reason for those judgments, his appraisals might be indistinguishable from those of someone following the mixed conception. *There is, I assume, sufficient latitude in the determination of the level of the social minimum under varying conditions to bring about this result.*[47]

What does Rawls mean by saying that "there is sufficient latitude in the determination of the social minimum?" First, that given the similarity already apparent between his two principles and a mixed conception of justice, both alternatives will recommend similar institutional arrangements. Second, that these institutional arrangements are likely to lead to roughly the same results. He tries to establish these conclusions by arguing that institutions under either alternative can be arranged to distribute benefits widely, keep inequalities within narrow bounds, and serve efficiency. In other words, Rawls believes that the "general facts of social theory" show that the requirements of efficiency and equality do not conflict as sharply as many have thought. If so, then the parties can be assured that *both* alternatives will produce satisfactory outcomes under "reasonably favorable" conditions. The function of a theory of institutions in Rawls's theory, therefore, is not to decide between these two alternatives, but to show that neither of them is likely to generate the counterintuitive outcomes that Rae and Fishkin believe will arise. And this changes the problem of choice in the original position. For if we assume that both conceptions of justice are in this sense feasible, the question is whether one of them is relatively more precise.

These empirical assumptions are of course problematic. Leaving them aside for the moment, however, let us focus instead on the question of relative precision. For it is here that we finally reach Rawls's deepest understanding of the question we have been considering all along. Assuming that Rawls's institutional theory is defensible, how are the parties to settle this question? We might think that the way to decide this issue is by seeing which conception of justice more exactly matches our considered judgments about a satisfactory welfare floor and the relative claims of intermediate social groups. On this view, one conception of justice is preferable to another if it more closely approximates our intuitive sense of justice: in this sense, it is more "precise." Rawls appears to reject this view, however, when, in the Dewey Lectures, for example, he says that his two principles are "not regarded as a workable approximation to the moral facts: there are no moral facts to which the principles adopted to could approximate."[48]

Rawls's various remarks in the Dewey Lectures can easily be interpreted as announcing a radical epistemological thesis: we are free to make up whatever principles of justice we want, since there is no "truth of the matter" that can serve as an independent standard for our activity.[49] There is also a more moderate interpretation of these Lectures, however. On this interpretation, Rawls is only pointing out that our ordinary experience offers no clear perspective on the problem of balancing first principles, given the size and complexity of the basic structure as a whole. As Nozick remarks, "There are special disadvantages to proceeding by focusing only on the intuitive justice of described complex wholes. For complex wholes are not easily scanned: we cannot easily keep track of everything that is relevant."[50] Under these circumstances, pluralism tells us to strike a balance between "aggregate welfare" and "greater equality in the distribution of satisfaction." But who among us is in a position to give the correct answer to this problem, much less explain its basis? There is no definite answer to a question of this sort: how could there be? As Rawls says, these notions are too abstract and comprehensive to understand. Given this reading of the problem, we must devise a theory of justice that lets us

> decide the best way to fill out our conceptions of justice. . . . The two principles may not so much oppose our intuitive convictions as provide a relatively concrete principle for questions that common sense finds unfamiliar and leaves undecided. Thus, while the difference principle strikes us as strange at first, reflection on its implications *when it is suitably circumscribed* may convince us that it . . . *projects* our (considered) judgments in an acceptable way.[51]

These remarks explain why Rawls is not prepared to drop his contractarian argument in favor an argument for first principles under conditions of full information. For this more conventional approach to social justice merely brings back the problem we are trying to solve. Asked to explain how we set a welfare floor by intuition, all we can say is that one solution accords better with our considered judgments than another, which seems to be no explanation at all. We therefore lack a public standard of justification that we can appeal to when our intuitions conflict. Justice as fairness, on the other hand, connects the difference principle to a philosophical argument that is quite general. It gives deeper intelligibility to what would otherwise appear to be merely a series of ad hoc judgments. It is a mistake, then, to think of the difference principle as approximating some prior standard of justice. The difference principle is instead a decision-rule that we devise in the absence of any other nonabitrary way of resolving the balancing problem. Properly understood, Rawls's argument does not *discover* a more precise way of characterizing our sense of justice. Rather, it *creates* a degree of precision that was previously lacking. It is in this sense that the argument for the difference principle is primarily "practical," rather than "epistemological" in character.

Rawls's Theory of Institutions

Having sketched Rawls's new argument from the original position, we now come to its crux, his theory of institutions. And since the likely institutional implications of Rawls's two principles have been discussed almost as often the rest of his theory, I will be brief. Fortunately, previous discussions fall into a familiar pattern that can be easily summarized. Early critics found the institutional implications of Rawls's theory vague and controversial. Later commentators have offered a closer reading of his argument which shows that those implications are more definite than was originally thought. But although Rawls's institutional theory seems plausible, his overall argument remains inconclusive. We must now consider why this is necessarily so.

As Allan Buchanan observes, there are two ways that parties to the social contract might try to determine the institutional requirements of Rawls's two principles.[52] Behind the full veil of ignorance, it seems they must choose principles in the light of all *logically possible* institutional arrangements that might be compatible with their decision. This choice is imponderable. Alternatively, they might assume that since the selection of principles takes place under "reasonably favorable" conditions, the range of institutional structures can be narrowed by looking at only those institutions that are in some sense feasible granted certain empirical features of societies roughly like our own. It is this second alternative that Rawls apparently has in mind:

Which of these systems and the many intermediate forms most fully
answers to the requirements of justice cannot, I think, be determined in
advance. There is presumably no general answer to this question, since
it depends on the traditions, institutions and social forces of each country,
and its historical circumstances. The theory of justice does not include
these matters. But what it can do is set out in a schematic way the
outlines of a just economic system that admits of several variations. The
political judgments in any case will then turn on which variation is most
likely to work out in practice. A conception of justice is a necessary part
of any such political assessment, but it is not sufficient.[53]

Unfortunately, this strategy has its own problems. As Buchanan remarks, constructing a set of institutional alternatives relative to our
present traditions and circumstances may make our notions of what is
feasible too dependent upon existing injustices.[54] For this reason, early
critics found the purported institutional implications of Rawls's principles either question begging or unacceptably vague.

Later commentators have shown, however, that the implications of
Rawls's theory are more definite than might first appear. For example,
it is now clear that there are several social systems that Rawls's two
principles *rule out*. His original argument did not logically exclude
slavery. But his recent emphasis on a particular ideal of the person
now makes that alternative a complete nonstarter. The question of
whether Rawls's two principles permit capitalism, that is, a rigid class
structure characterized by unproductive ownership of wealth, might
seem more controversial. But as Arthur di Quattro has recently pointed
out, this term in fact never appears once in *A Theory of Justice*.[55] When
Rawls turns to the question of how the two principles might be worked
out, he instead describes a "property-owning democracy." In a regime
of this sort inequalities are limited in several ways: by a requirement
that we preserve the "fair value" of liberty; by insuring fair equality
of opportunity; by widely distributing ownership in investment trusts
and insurance firms so that each person derives partial income from
property; and, perhaps most importantly, by using a wide variety of
educational and job training programs to enlarge the supply of skilled
labor, thereby guaranteeing that no more economic rent is paid on
scarce talents than is absolutely necessary.[56] Although Rawls does rely
heavily on markets, he distinguishes sharply between their allocative
and distributive functions: The purpose of the market is to compensate
individuals for their costs in contributing to the common good and to
insure allocative efficiency, not to reward unproductive ownership.[57]

Of course, both slavery and capitalism might be defended as a matter
of *nonideal* theory, by showing that under some historical circumstances

they are less unjust than the available alternatives.[58] But neither of these social systems can be defended from the perspective of *ideal* theory, for the simple reason that there is nothing in "the general facts of social theory" that demonstrates their continuing *necessity*. In other words, "feasibility," in the weak sense of "logical and empirical possibility," is a notion that does more work in Rawls's theory than early commentators were willing to grant. In order to argue against slavery and capitalism, all that he must show is that these systems license inequalities that do not contribute to the least-advantaged and that the eventual replacement of these social systems is not literally impossible.

This still leaves the question, however, of which institutional arrangements ideal theory *permits*. And here there are two difficulties. The first difficulty was discussed earlier: implementation of the difference principle at various stages of Rawls's "four-stage sequence" is often indeterminate, given the continuing controversy over the general facts of social theory. As he says, this sort of indeterminacy is not itself a defect; it is what we should expect. But as I pointed out earlier, Rawls now asks the parties simply to defer a number of additional difficulties, such as the problem of constructing a complete index of primary goods for normal individuals and the issue of special needs. The parties in the original position can have little assurance that they will be able to settle these problems at later stages. Thus, the process of implementing the difference principle is more uncertain than Rawls originally allowed.

The second difficulty is even more serious. Not only do Rawls's two principles often fail to determine the particular policies that will be chosen at each stage of his four-stage sequence, but they also fail to determine the rate of reform.[59] This is a crucial problem, both for ideal and nonideal theory. The difference principle states that basic inequalities should be arranged to the "long-run" advantage of the least well-off. But this formulation conceals the trade-offs involved in deciding how far the "long-run" extends, given the existing incentive structures that come to light when the veil of ignorance is lifted. Presumably, there are variety of paths to full implementation of the difference principle over time. Even if the parties possessed a social science with perfect predictive powers, therefore, the problem of balancing the relative benefits and burdens of various reform strategies over time would remain.

These two problems show why the choice between Rawls's two principles and a pluralistic conception of justice remains moot. For all of the balancing problems that Rawls hoped to banish reappear, once it is recognized that the difference principle must be put into effect over the long run. Rawls's project, after all, is to replace an ongoing *moral* argument about where to set the minimum and how to treat the expectations of intermediate social groups with a set of *technical* arguments about how to reach an agreed-upon end, namely, the long-run advantage of the least well-off. We do not thereby eliminate political disagreement completely, but we do provide a public standard that is not itself in question when we try to settle our most basic disputes. In other words, the purpose of finding an alternative to pluralism is to transform political arguments so that they are largely about means rather than ends. At a certain point, however, we can no longer convincingly argue that disagreement about how to implement the difference principle is merely a disagreement about means. At a certain point, disagreement about the means to a given end must be regarded as disagreement about the meaning of that end itself, and this is what happens to the difference principle.

When we ask how the difference principle is to be implemented over time, we are told only that we must somehow strike a balance between equality and efficiency in the interim. The difference principle itself provides no guidance to this problem: we must fall back on intuition. At the same time, the goal of complete implementation recedes steadily on the horizon, since, of course, individuals continue to change and adapt to each new attempt to put the principle into effect. The relative precision of the difference principle turns out, then, to be largely illusory: at best the locus of political disagreement has been shifted without modifying or eliminating it. Indeed, under these circumstances a mixed conception of justice might seem preferable, for pluralism recognizes that in trying to implement the difference principle over the long run, we are in fact always balancing distributive and aggregative considerations and choosing policies on the basis of intuition.

Would this objection disappear if we could confidently predict the results of different social and economic policies in advance? To put the question another way, does Rawls's approach at least remain important in a programmatic sense, even though his own argument remains unpersuasive? Many theorists would appear to think so, particularly those on the political left. Buchanan, for example, believes that Rawls's general approach needs to be supplemented by a "theory of transition," which would "allow us to take the nature of current motivational structures and the limitations they place on productivity into account, while at the same time explaining how these limitations can and will be transcended."[60] A theory of this sort would show that full implementation of the difference principle need not prove continually elusive and would therefore lend some credibility to the idea of a politics that is primarily concerned with means rather than ends.

Our evaluation of the programmatic significance of Rawls's institutional strategy depends to a large extent on our view of the prospects of eventually achieving a social science of the sort that Buchanan imagines, for as Bedau observes, the ultimate success of Rawls's approach depends on our ability to discover law-like generalizations about what human conduct would be like in the absence of actual basic institutions and the presence of others.[61] And since this question threatens to take us far afield, I will limit myself to two observations.

The first thing to be remarked, of course, is that we are still very far from achieving the kind of social theory that Buchanan envisions. More importantly, the prospects for achieving law-like generalizations about human conduct have begun to look exceedingly dim, although perhaps still not impossible in principle. It may prove possible to state the necessary conditions for the establishment and maintenance of certain basic institutions. But in the last three decades, critical discussion of positivism in the social sciences has made the project of stating necessary and sufficient conditions for institutional change appear naive. Any attempt to explain the thoughts, beliefs, and conduct of individuals strictly in terms of various background practices and institutions must ignore the ways in which such institutions and practices are always partially constituted by what people think and feel about them.[62] And these self-understandings are themselves continually changing in a way that in turn transforms the context that was supposed to provide the explanation. As Charles Taylor has remarked, "Really to be able to predict the future would be to have explicated so clearly the human condition that one would already have pre-empted all cultural innovation and transformation. This is hardly in the bounds of the possible."[63] Moreover, even if we did achieve a "theory of transition" that could predict how "existing motivational structures can and will be overcome," this would still not settle the normative problem of choosing between different ways of achieving the difference principle over the long run. For again, there is presumably more than one feasible path to this goal. Add to these difficulties the fact that the indexing problem is itself a political rather than technical problem, and it becomes even more apparent why the prospects of reducing politics to a debate over means appears unlikely.

To Rawls's credit, he has recognized that the above sources of indeterminacy are likely to leave most questions of social and economic justice to "quasi-pure" procedural justice even in the long run. In contrast with other recent theorists, it is also to his credit that his empirical assumptions are at least relevant to questions that are actually likely to arise in practice. For example, he assumes that social cooperation is fruitful and productive, rather than imagining a manna economy or a desert island situation in which all economic activity is a zero-sum game.[64] But uncertainty about the empirical effects of different social and economic policies makes the operational meaning of his principles very hard to determine. And this is not merely a limitation of Rawls's own particular theory. *Any* theory of justice for the basic structure must rely on such assumptions if it is to overcome the difficulties raised by Fishkin and Rae. But this means that any such theory faces the problems outlined above.

Implicit in the idea of the basic structure as subject, finally, is a metaphor that needs to be uncovered. The idea of the basic structure suggests the view that society is like a machine. The imagery of the basic structure is mechanical: We set up a certain set of institutional arrangements and through the operation of pure procedural justice a certain range of results is automatically generated. If we know the general mechanics of these institutions they can be adjusted to produce results falling within satisfactory limits, which are determined in advance by the expectations of various social positions. The idea of a theory of institutions also suggests the idea of a mechanics, which tells us how to organize all of the parts of a machine so that it runs smoothly and generates the intended result.[65] To really be able to make this approach to the problem of social justice work, however, we would have to know much more about the outputs that various basic structures will produce than we in fact do, or are ever likely to.

Without this information, the question is how far we should take Rawls's mechancial metaphor in the first place. To be sure, he does not take it as far as the utilitarians, since he rejects the idea that the purpose of social cooperation is merely the efficient coordination of social activity in pursuit of a single collective end. As Rawls says, the purposes of social cooperation in a liberal society must instead be understood as one of "mutual advantage," where individuals' final aims are assumed to be incommensurable from the beginning.[66] Nevertheless, the idea of coordinating each separate sphere of distribution in society in order to achieve a single outcome is still present in a limited form in Rawls's theory. It appears most clearly in the idea of an index of primary goods, which allows us to assess the overall standing of at least one particular group. This is no doubt a much easier problem than trying to measure the overall standing of each particular member of society, yet it still requires us to coordinate what happens in the schools, the markets, the political arena, and the family in order to insure that all basic social and economic inequalities are arranged to the benefit of the least well-off. The burden of this chapter has been that the sort of precision presupposed by this aim is beyond our powers. Not only does the problem of defining an index in some uncontroversial way seem impossible to solve, but, even if we had such an index, we could not have enough confidence in how the difference principle might affect individuals and intermediate groups over time to know whether we ought to accept it.

Of course, this still leaves us with the problem of determining the degree of precision we should expect from a theoretical discussion of social justice. And since Rawls has understood the difficulties of achieving an appropriate degree of precision better than any other recent theorist, it is worth reviewing that understanding here. Rawls rejects commonsense principles of justice because they are at the wrong level of generality and ignore the importance of "background" justice. He rejects philosophical first principles, such as utility and equality in the distribution of satisfaction, because, while at the right level of generality, they are too abstract and comprehensive to interpret. And he rejects attempts to determine the standing of each particular member of society according to some measure of overall individual equality because such attempts generate unworkable complexities and ultimately make no sense. His rejection of each of these ways of theorizing about social justice is quite sensible. Unfortunately, Rawls's own approach of combining a simple end-state principle with a theory of institutions also fails.

There remains, however, one difference between the first approach that Rawls rejects and all of the others. We at least know what we are talking about when we discuss social justice at the level of commonsense pluralism and even at the level of what Rawls calls a pluralism of social ends. Beyond this point, we quickly begin to lose our grasp of what is supposedly under discussion, as Rawls observes. He argues that we must either take the basic structure as subject or else ignore the importance of "background justice." Although this conclusion is to a certain extent correct, the alternatives are posed too starkly. The alternative to dropping the idea of the basic structure, understood as a single, global unit of analysis, is not one of ignoring background injustice altogether. Rather, what we must give up is the idea of redressing the effects of background injustice all at once, from some comprehensive perspective. Of course, many theorists have resisted this conclusion. For that reason, my final chapter considers some of the objections that have been raised against commonsense pluralism in more detail.

NOTES

1. Rawls, "Kantian Constructivism in Moral Theory," p. 570.
2. For Rawls's discussion of pluralism, which he calls "intuitionism," see *A Theory of Justice*, pp. 35-36.
3. Ibid., p. 44.
4. Barry, *The Liberal Theory of Justice*, p. 43 (emphasis added).
5. Dworkin, "Equality of Resources," pp. 343-44.
6. Gutmann, *Liberal Equality*, p. 126.
7. Pogge, *Kant, Rawls, and Global Justice*, pp. 125-35.
8. Rawls, "The Basic Liberties and Their Priority," p. 6.
9. Ibid., p. 10.
10. Pogge, *Kant, Rawls, and Global Justice*, p. 135.
11. Gutmann, *Liberal Equality*, p. 126; also, p. 256, n. 30.
12. Ibid., p. 127.
13. Rawls, *A Theory of Justice*, p. 7.
14. Beauchamp, "Distributive Justice and the Difference Principle," p. 158.
15. Ibid.
16. Rawls, *A Theory of Justice*, p. 201.
17. Rawls, "Social Unity and Primary Goods," p. 168.
18. Ibid., n. 8.
19. Rawls, "Fairness to Goodness," p. 539.
20. For a more detailed discussion, see Daniels, "Health Care Needs and Distributive Justice," p. 171.
21. Ibid., p. 149.
22. Ibid.
23. For a good summary of the difficulties, see Barber, "Justifying Justice: Problems of Psychology, Politics and Measurement in Rawls," pp. 663-74.
24. Rawls, *A Theory of Justice*, p. 157.
25. Ibid., p. 87.
26. Nozick, *Anarchy, State, and Utopia*, p. 202.
27. Rae, "A Principle of Simple Justice," p. 152.
28. Ibid.
29. Fishkin, *Justice, Equal Opportunity, and the Family*, p. 19.
30. Rae, "Maximin Justice and an Alternative Principle of General Advantage," p. 643.
31. Rawls, *A Theory of Justice*, p. 44.
32. Ibid., p. 157.
33. Ibid., p. 153.
34. Rawls, "Social Unity and Primary Goods," p. 159.
35. Ibid., pp. 180-81.
36. Ibid., p. 180.
37. Ibid., p. 159.
38. Nagel, "Rawls on Justice," in Daniels, ed., *Reading Rawls*, p. 11.
39. Rawls, "Kantian Constructivism," p. 549.

40. Rawls, "The Basic Liberties and Their Priority," p. 11.

41. Ibid., p. 26.

42. Strasnick, p. 508.

43. Rawls, "Social Unity and Primary Goods," p. 170.

44. Strasnick, p. 508.

45. Ibid., p. 509.

46. Rawls, *A Theory of Justice*, p. 318.

47. Ibid., pp. 316-17 (emphasis added).

48. Rawls, "Kantian Constructivism," p. 564.

49. Rawls denies that any aspect of his method of justification corresponds to the notion of 'radical choice' associated with Nietzsche and the existentialists. See "Kantian Constructivism in Moral Theory," pp. 568-69.

50. Nozick, *Anarchy, State, and Utopia*, p. 205.

51. Rawls, *A Theory of Justice*, p. 319 (emphasis added).

52. Buchanan, *Marx and Justice*, p. 126-27.

53. Rawls, *A Theory of Justice*, p. 274.

54. Ibid.

55. di Quattro, "Rawls and Left Criticism," p. 56.

56. Ibid., pp. 56-78.

57. Ibid., p. 69.

58. Ibid., p. 67.

59. For a representative example of this sort of criticism see Barber, "Justifying Justice: Problems of Psychology, Politics, and Measurement in Rawls," pp. 306-7.

60. Buchanan, *Marx and Justice*, p. 128.

61. Bedau, "Social Justice and Social Institutions," p. 168.

62. See MacIntyre, *Against the Self-Images of the Age*, p. 247.

63. Taylor, "Interpretation and the Sciences of Man," p. 130.

64. Rawls, "Kantian Constructivism," p. 536.

65. "The lawgiver is the engineer who invents the machine; the prince is merely the mechanic who sets it up and operates it." Rousseau, *The Social Contract*, p. 84.

66. Rawls, "Social Unity and Primary Goods," p. 184.

CHAPTER 7

Conclusion

In Chapters 2 through 5, I considered several recent theories of social justice that try to provide standards for making comprehensive comparisons of the overall situations of each member of society. In the last chapter, I considered Rawls's theory of justice, which has the relatively more modest aim of defining social justice in terms of the expectations of two "representative positions." Neither approach has proved satisfactory. The first kind of theory has turned out to be either senseless or unworkably complex. The second simplified the problem of social justice, but still failed to reach a determinate conception of justice for the basic structure as a whole. But if we can neither add up all of the different ways in which specific individuals might be advantaged and disadvantaged, nor construct an index from all of the different sorts of resources that might be relevant to assessing the position of the "least well-off," we seem to have reached a dead end. On the basis of this survey, we might be pardoned for thinking that for over fifteen years now, theorists of justice have largely wasted their efforts.

This conclusion would be mistaken, however. Political theorists have made progress over the last fifteen years, especially in developing a richer and more varied account of basic rights and in providing a number of overlapping arguments for what Rawls calls "the fair value" of the political liberties. What has failed is the underlying project of establishing the priority of the basic liberties once and for all, along with the even more ambitious aim of developing a formula for measuring individual shares. This book is as much about the degree of precision that theorists of justice have aspired to as it is about the degree of precision they have achieved. Rawls, for example, fails to be as precise as he wishes. More importantly, however, his theory is ultimately unconvincing because he aspires to a degree of precision impossible to attain. What we need, then, is not to reject the work of contemporary theorists of social justice altogether but to reorient political theory in a more realistic direction. Within the discipline of political philosophy, we need to appreciate and respect the necessarily imprecise character of political debate.

To a certain extent, this reorientation is already taking place in the work of "communitarian" theorists such as Michael Sandel, Alasdair MacIntyre, Benjamin Barber, and especially Michael Walzer. From the perspective of this book, what unites these writers is their view that distributive goods are historical in character, heterogeneous, and thus incommensurable in terms of some more basic standard, such as overall equality. This is also the view of "commonsense pluralism" which holds that individual claims of need, desert, and entitlement arise in separate ways and in different contexts. Although these principles of need, desert, and entitlement stand in some general relation of decreasing importance, their relative weight in cases of conflict can ultimately be decided only by practical judgment. This limits our ability to deal with the question of background justice, and thus we can only redress the contingencies of nature and history in a rather piecemeal fashion.

What does it mean to say that a distributive good is historical in character? Walzer has stressed that even "necessary" goods, such as food, have a very different social significance at different times and places. Thus, "Bread is the staff of life, the body of Christ, the symbol of the Sabbath, the means of hospitality, and so on."[1] In Walzer's language, the historical or "social" meaning of a good already places it within a particular distributive context, or "sphere" of justice. Within classical Greek society, for example, the great drama festivals were understood as matters of religious education, and thus placed within the sphere of "communal welfare," where they were financed by taxation; in our society, theater is thought of as a commodity, and thus placed within the sphere of the "market," where tickets are bought and sold.[2] Within our own society, the meanings of goods have become increasingly distinct: religion and education, for example, are no longer tied together as they were in ancient Athens. Walzer argues that if we are to respect the distinct social meanings that have emerged within our own pluralistic society, our theory of justice must also be pluralistic. What we should aim at is "complex equality": no good, wealth for example, should be allowed to pattern or "dominate" the distribution of any other good, education or office for example. This ideal of "complex equality" between spheres of justice is radically different from Dworkin's idea of "complex equality" between individuals, first and foremost because it does not require a metric for commensurating individual claims to different kinds of goods. Walzer's ideal also addresses the objection that commonsense principles are at the wrong level of generality for a theory of "social" justice. Such precepts *are* too particular if we are attempting to coordinate the distribution of all social resources toward a single end. If our organizing principle for society as a whole is one of differentiation rather than coordination, these principles may well be general enough.

I will examine some of the difficulties with the idea of complex equality below. At this point, however, I wish to broaden my discussion. As usually presented, the communitarian position is associated with a set of deeper claims. Of course, "communitarianism," like "liberalism," is a term that refers to a variety of positions that bear only a family resemblance to one another. But given their skepticism about philosophy's ability to provide rules for balancing first principles, all communitarians agree that social justice must depend largely on the practical judgments of the community. Communitarians also agree with Michael Sandel that "we cannot justify political arrangements without reference to common ends and purposes, and that we cannot conceive of our personhood without reference to our role as citizens, and as participants in a common life."[3] Since communitarians hold that 'persons' are at least partially constituted by their membership within a particular community, they also generally maintain that it is membership within a particular community that ultimately confers rights, not vice versa. Liberals have found these views both vague and dangerous.

According to liberal critics, communitarian theories of justice are unacceptably vague because they make justice dependent on the "social meaning" of particular goods without explaining what counts as a better interpretation of the meaning of a good when such interpretations conflict. Communitarian theories of justice are dangerous because they do not firmly establish individual rights *against* the community. Finally, liberals have found the communitarian position self-contradictory, on the grounds that communitarians tend to condemn traditionally repressive societies while claiming that justice fundamentally consists in "a decent respect" for local traditions, whatever they may be.

Given the argument of this book, the importance of these objections is obvious. For it is precisely these objections to a more political or communal approach to questions of social justice that threaten to turn political theory back toward the sort of abstract theorizing that we should now leave behind. It is not enough, then, to show why the two kinds of theory examined in earlier chapters must fail. Unless we can also demonstrate that a more political approach to social justice is neither dangerous nor unacceptably vague, the impulse toward a more abstract kind of theorizing will persist.

I do not think, however, that the current debate between liberals and communitarians over the nature of moral personality sheds much light on these issues. Rather than taking sides in that controversy, therefore, I would like to focus once again on the theme of precision in a theory of justice in order to look at that debate from the outside, with more fruitful results. From this perspective, each side has failed to recognize what is useful in the other. For example, even if we accept the liberal claim that a theory of justice must begin with basic rights, we must still explain how such rights are further specified and balanced in one system and how other goods should be distributed. Quite apart from their deeper claims, it would appear that communitarians are correct in thinking that we cannot accomplish these tasks by reference to an abstract or liberal conception of the person alone. At the same time, however, it is crucial to reemphasize against communitarian critics that arguments based on an abstract conception of the person do not therefore suddenly become worthless. Quite the contrary: when citizens take up the more detailed and specific questions that theorists of justice have thus far tackled in vain, they can and should draw on such arguments in justifying a framework for political debate about justice. In other words, the current debate between liberals and communitarians obscures much of the progress that has been made. At least with regard to both a framework of basic rights and a principle for distributing political power, there is actually a great deal of agreement about what justice requires.

This way of viewing the current debate in political theory also allows us to be more precise about areas of continuing disagreement, thereby making the reorientation of political philosophy suggested above more concrete. "Communitarians" of course argue that community is prior to justice in the sense that claims of justice can only arise between individuals whose identities are already at least partly constituted by their membership. But since "we" already live within a society that is deeply committed to a view of the person and a set of practices that support the idea of rights, this deeper communitarian claim may end up making little substantive difference for us. Instead, the central issue separating most contemporary theorists of justice concerns the extension of a particular, participatory ideal of community to the sphere of politics and, beyond that, to other distributive contexts *within* our framework of basic rights, or so I will argue. Given our concerns, the advantage of the communitarian ideal of participation is that it provides an additional, external standard to which to appeal when social meanings are in dispute, thereby partly meeting the objection that a more political approach to social justice is unacceptably vague. However, I argue that there are good reasons for refusing to follow those communitarian theorists who have suggested that this standard will serve to resolve all of our disagreements about social justice. Rather, this participatory ideal raises a new set of questions that political theorists must now address.

In what follows, then, I will show that we can bring the work of recent theorists of justice together in a way that justifies a basic framework of rights and a particular understanding of democratic politics. Debate over the social meaning of particular goods may break down, however, so I also try to show that when we reach an impasse we can appeal to a particular ideal of community as an additional standard. Finally, I will suggest that there are indeed cases in which there is "no right answer" to questions about distributive justice. But by the time we confront this possibility it should be apparent that the charges above have been exaggerated. We do not need to return to a more abstract mode of theorizing about justice in order to avoid the dangers that supposedly accompany a pluralist view.

Justifying Basic Rights

Since there are a variety of communitarian views about rights, it will be helpful at the outset to distinguish strong and weak versions of the communitarian critique. In the strong version, natural or human rights are regarded as a fiction, since all attempts to demonstrate their existence have failed. In particular, it is argued that absent the appropriate practices or institutions, the very idea of such rights lacks sense. In societies without the necessary institutional context, claiming a human right would be "like presenting a check for payment in a social order that lacked the institution of money."[4] By contrast, in the weak version of the communitarian position the existence of human rights to life and liberty is taken for granted. Nevertheless, such rights are "only of limited help in thinking about distributive justice. . . . The effort to produce a complete account of justice or a defense of equality by multiplying rights soon makes a farce of what it multiplies."[5] Beyond life and liberty, then, whatever rights we have depend on communal membership and shared understandings of social goods. Corresponding to these two formulations of the communitarian position are two versions of the liberal response. The strong version of the liberal position reasserts the possibility of demonstrating the existence of human rights and usually cites the work of Alan Gewirth as evidence that this task has already been accomplished.[6] The weak version, on the other hand, acknowledges the force of contextualist arguments against the idea of human rights but notes that in our society practices necessary to the idea of basic rights already exist.[7]

In general, the strong liberal response has focused on the apparent contradiction in the communitarian position mentioned at the outset of this chapter. Historically, we are acquainted with communities that have conceived of persons in a way that makes widespread repression of critical thought perfectly respectable. This has often been the case when the purpose of individual existence has been understood primarily as one of obedience to divine commands or subservience to the mission of the collectivity. Liberal critics point out, however, that modern communitarians generally wish to make room for dissent even within such traditions. For example, Alasdair MacIntyre has maintained that a tradition is only in "good order" when it is "partially constituted by an *argument* about the goods the pursuit of which gives to that tradition its particular point and purpose."[8] Thus, communitarians appear to want it both ways at once, embracing the idea of tradition as the basis of moral judgment, yet criticizing particular traditions whenever they conflict with a liberal conception of the person.

Unfortunately, this sort of criticism fails to establish the strong version of the liberal position. It is one thing to show that most communitarians implicitly accept and valorize a view of persons as at least potentially rational and autonomous (they clearly do). It is quite another to show that this conception of the person is or should be regarded as more than the common heritage of all Western post-Enlightenment thinkers, whether liberal *or* communitarian. In judging the moral practices of other societies, it is of course impossible not to presuppose some basis for judgment. But this does not show that our basis for judgment has the standing that the strong liberal response would assign to it. To establish this conclusion, liberals must provide an independent set of arguments. To the extent that liberals have tried to do so, however, it is by falling back the project of deducing a set of rights from a concept of the person as a "prudential," that is, rationally self-interested agent. There are many well-known difficulties with this project, however, several of which are raised again by communitarian writers. In particular, the view that freedom and well-being are necessary conditions of agency does not entail the conclusion that rights are the only rational way of securing freedom and well-being. A society without the device of rights might in some circumstances secure the necessary conditions of agency just as well, if not better. If this kind of argument provides the best foundation for the strong liberal response, that response is doubtful at best.[9]

Let us assume, however, that we *can* deduce a set of basic rights from the notion of the person as rational agent. Even if it can be shown that certain rights necessarily flow from this idea of the person, and even if such rights justify some redistribution within a particular community, they do not do so as a matter of social justice. For whatever else they might be, rights of social justice are *social*, that is, they arise by virtue of some prior cooperative relationship. The rights we are concerned with now are human rights, however, which exist regardless of any prior relationship. We might put the weak communitarian response more strongly, then: it is not merely that the idea of human rights would not end up doing much work in a theory of social justice, but rather that such rights by definition cannot.

Failure to make this basic distinction between kinds of rights has been a source of considerable confusion.[10] Since this may appear to be a quibble about definitions, however, we should also note that even on the most generous reading of theorists such as Gewirth, arguments about "the necessary conditions of rational agency" will yield only negative rights against coercion and positive rights to the satisfaction of a minimal set of "basic needs." Beyond this point, we are concerned with resources that are of variable and controversial worth *to* agents rather than necessary logical and empirical conditions *of* agency. Very little is required for someone to exercise agency, and the attempt to extend this argument in order to generate rights to "the equal worth" of the conditions of agency must introduce controversial assumptions about the relative worth of the ends of action. Certainly the idea of rational agency cannot be used to derive anything as substantive as a right to a specific kind of polity such as liberal democracy. At best, the rights we can justify will include the liberty and integrity of the person, freedom of thought and conscience, freedom of association, and the rule of law.

For these reasons, the weak liberal response begins by simply assuming a much more substantive conception of the person as the foundation of a theory of justice. Justice as fairness, for example, has been relativized to certain ideals of social cooperation and moral personality assumed to be implicit in the culture of a modern, liberal democratic society. Rawlsians concede, at least for "practical" purposes, the strong version of the communitarian critique, but ask what difference that critique makes in developing a theory of justice for us. And given the multiple difficulties of the strong version of the liberal position, I believe it is only at this point that the real issues are first joined. I have already argued in Chapter 6, however, that this more substantive conception of the person (in conjunction with the original position) is inadequate to determine how social and economic resources should be distributed. Thus, it remains only to ask whether the priority of the basic civil and political liberties can be justified on this basis. If they cannot, then we need not examine whether an explanation can also be given as to how to arrange the basic liberties in one system. Failure to justify the priority of liberty will show that the later stages of Rawls's argument require more information than the original position allows.

It cannot be doubted that in the Tanner Lectures, Rawls has presented one of the most powerful and systematic defenses of the basic liberties to date. Given our stipulated interest in exercising our "two moral powers," Rawls has shown there are several independent justifications for each of the basic liberties (which include freedom of expression, the political liberties, and the right to hold some property) and that those justifications are mutually reinforcing when we consider the basic liberties as one system. Nevertheless, the Tanner Lectures do not accomplish Rawls's aim. The same difficulty that has dogged Rawls from the start—the imponderable nature of the choice in the original position—still remains. In the original position it must be rational to give priority to all of the liberties mentioned above, whatever the circumstances, provided now that those circumstances are assumed to be reasonably favorable. But of course this last phrase begs all of the questions. Can it be rational to agree to the *absolute* priority of these liberties (or believe that they can be regulated in one system) without knowing anything, for example, about the degree and intensity of religious belief in our society? If we do know that in our society the state of religious tolerance is reasonably favorable, what does this mean? Isn't this exactly the sort of circumstance that we must discuss, debate, and evaluate in order to decide whether the priority of liberty *is* rational? Or to take another example, what about our relationships with other societies? Can we agree that there should be no prior restraint of the press (even a quite temporary one) without knowing anything about potential or actual threats to national security? In general, would it be rational to insist on the priority of the basic liberties in all cases without having any idea about how enforcing those liberties might affect our other loyalties and attachments? It must be remembered that if there is *any* contingent situation in which it might be reasonable to limit the basic liberties for the sake of other some other goal, Rawls's argument fails.

Someone wishing to defend a Rawlsian view might respond to the criticism above by claiming that it *is* rational for the parties to agree to the priority of liberty even though they do not know exactly what the phrase "reasonably favorable conditions" means. He might argue that our highest order interest in the exercise of our two moral powers results in the priority of liberty being preferable under practically any set of conditions. However, we must not forget that the purpose of

Rawls's theory is to provide authoritative standards for resolving controversies that we cannot now settle. As a minimum, then, Rawls must specify "reasonably favorable conditions" for the priority of liberty in a way that is independent of current controversies about when such conditions exist. If he does not, the choice of the parties in the original position will be biased in a way that begs the sort of questions that Rawls's argument is meant to resolve. This problem is itself serious enough, but an even more serious difficulty has yet to be mentioned. Principles chosen in the original position are intended to be binding for the future as well as the present. If Rawls is to avoid begging the question, then, his description of "reasonably favorable conditions" must not rule prematurely on controversies that might arise about the reasonableness of those conditions. It is difficult to see how this can be done, since we might always change our minds about conditions that we now find reasonable enough.

In reply to this new difficulty, a Rawlsian might repond that a well ordered society is stable, in the sense that once the priority of liberty is settled there is a psychological tendency against reopening questions about the priority of liberty. The evidence for this proposition is tenuous, however. On the one hand, our society is by hypothesis not well ordered. Evidence drawn from this source is inherently suspect. On the other hand, this is the only sort of evidence we have, and, in commenting on our own history of constitutional interpretation, Rawls gives examples of repeated attempts to compromise the basic liberties.

More generally, we again confront the problem discussed in Chapter 6: Background institutions and practices that supposedly explain human conduct are themselves partially constituted by the self-understandings of human beings, and those self-understandings can and do change in apparently unpredictable ways. From this perspective it is *impossible* to specify the meaning of "reasonably favorable conditions" behind the veil of ignorance. For example, if the parties are told that the intensity of religious belief in their society is low enough to make the priority of liberty feasible, this description presupposes that we have reliable empirical generalizations about the relationship between religious intensity and the political stability of a liberal society. But if human beings change over time in ways that make the reliability of such generalizations questionable, how are we to describe the circumstances of choice in a way that allows the parties to choose wisely for the future? It seems that we must be able to make reliable empirical generalizations about the reliability of our empirical generalizations, and so on.[11]

If we are skeptical about the liberal argument at this point, however, an obvious but apparently overlooked conclusion follows. That arguments drawn from this yet more substantive conception of the person fail by themselves to place a definite and more specific set of rights on an unquestionable footing does not mean that such arguments suddenly become negligible. Rather, their *philosophical* failure at the level of the original position means that they must now be seen as arguments that citizens can draw upon in *political* debate about what social justice requires under conditions of full information. Consider, for example, Rawls's argument in the Tanner Lectures that freedom of conscience may be regarded as both instrumentally important because it allows us to revise our conception of the good and intrinsically important because the process of revising our conception of the good may itself be part of our conception of the good. Such arguments do not show that liberty of conscience should be maintained under all circumstances (unless we add the question-begging ceteris paribus clause). In other words, these arguments must be regarded as political in the sense that they are less than conclusive in all circumstances and must therefore be employed in conjunction with (or in opposition to) arguments based on particular understandings of other social goods and their relative urgency. Detached from the philosophical aim of establishing the absolute priority of liberty, however, the sort of considerations adduced by Rawls in favor of the basic liberties still provide strong reasons for according them great importance, and, *in most circumstances*, will prove conclusive. It is crucial to such arguments, however, that we know what those circumstances are.

When it is asked, then, what citizens will say to each other when they discuss the sort of questions that philosophers have failed to resolve, it must be remembered that citizens are asking a different sort of question than philosophers and demanding a different, and less certain, kind of answer.[12] The questions asked by citizens are quite a bit more circumstantial: What set of rights is justified given the interests, beliefs, values, and historical experience of this particular society? Nevertheless, with respect to many fundamental questions (e.g., whether we should favor constitutional guarantees for freedom of conscience) the answers are relatively settled. This point would perhaps be too obvious to make if liberals weren't so worried about the prospect of returning questions about the specific weights and contours of rights to politics. Given that worry, however, the point bears repeating: there are many familiar, strong, and overlapping arguments available for the basic liberties. This is not to deny that Rawls and others have accomplished a great deal by giving those arguments a deeper and more systematic expression. But Rawls did not invent these arguments de novo even if the original position does provide a novel way of representing them, and the arguments that Rawls has presented are not by themselves decisive in every circumstance we can imagine (unless, again, we add the qualification that spoils everything). Communitarians are correct that the justification of the basic liberties must itself be more circumstantial and therefore more political, that is, less certain than many liberals would like. But it cannot be doubted that the arguments that Rawls advances appeal to convictions that are deeply embedded in our culture. There is little reason to believe that the resulting framework for political debate will be dramatically different if we retain those arguments for the basic liberties but divorce them from the attempt to achieve the kind of precision that Rawls and other theorists of justice would like. More importantly, detaching those arguments from this quest for an impossible degree of precision does not mean that political justice has suddenly been equated in some crude way with "whatever the community likes."

Democratic Politics

In order to sketch a political framework for discussing social justice, it is necessary to show that liberals and communitarians are and should be in general agreement about principles for the distribution of political power as well as rights. And once again, we can begin by distinguishing strong and weak versions of the communitarian position. The strong communitarian argument for distributing political power on the basis of participation rests on the view that political life is a preeminent good for autonomous citizens and indeed that participation and autonomy are inseparable. It is through participation, and particularly through what Benjamin Barber calls "strong democratic talk," that "we constantly reencounter, reevaluate, and repossess the beliefs, principles and maxims on the basis of which we exert our will in the political realm. To be free, it is not enough for us simply to will what we choose to will. We must will what truly belongs to us."[13]

According to the strong communitarian position, democratic debate forces individuals to defend and justify their beliefs; this demand for justification reveals that we are often mistaken, helps us to think for ourselves, improves our empathy with others, and teaches respect for those with whom we continue to differ; this increased humility, personal autonomy, and respect for others in turn makes our search for agreement less adversarial and potentially more successful. Participatory democracy makes a shared understanding of justice possible by allowing citizens to hammer out an agreement about justice together.

Thus, democratic community appears as a precondition of justice. At the same time, as a sense of democratic community increases, the demands of justice become less important, since the friends of a democratic community do not stand on their rights. Thus, democratic community also appears as an ideal beyond justice. In other words, the strong communitarian position maintains that autonomy, justice, and community are dialectically interrelated. Moreover, instead of being used as a vague synonym for a sense of "belonging" or psychological connectedness, community is now defined in terms of particular participatory ideal. Our aim is to make political society resemble a discussion among friends (or at least among friendly adversaries), and the degree of community can be assessed by the intensity of democratic participation and discussion.

As presented, however, this general argument concerns the transformative virtues of a certain kind of participation in any setting. It suggests that if we are to reorient our approach to justice by emphasizing social meanings, then we will want to democratize not just politics, but other spheres of justice as well, so that meanings will indeed become shared as they are jointly and self-consciously determined. But while this strong version of the communitarian position will be important later on, we can reach the same principle for the distribution of political power by means of a weaker formulation that postpones many of the difficulties. And of course the strong communitarian position does face many difficulties. To mention just a few: The scale and complexity of modern societies makes the ideal of widespread participation seem unrealistic. Given the size of the modern state, it is unlikely that most citizens will in fact regard participation as a preeminent good. Increased participation at the local level may intensify conflicts with groups in other localities while simultaneously weakening identification with the community at the national level. Given the social pluralism of our society, political debate may fail to be "transformative" at all, and instead merely intensify conflict.[14] More important, perhaps, than these difficulties, which strong communitarians clearly appreciate, are several potential conflicts between autonomy and freedom, two different values which communitarians often seem to conflate. Attempts to strengthen autonomy can and often do conflict with freedom, as the example of compulsory schooling clearly illustrates. At an even deeper level, *both* communitarians and liberals assume that persons are rational agents capable of participation. Strengthening a sense of *democratic* membership, therefore, may make it conceptually and psychologically easier to exclude those who are marginal by virtue of their inability to participate or even to act as agents (e.g. drug addicts, the severely handicapped).[15]

Given these problems, it is important to see that communitarians and liberals can still agree on the same principle for the distribution of political power itself, without necessarily agreeing on the extent of political participation that is desirable. For even if such participation *cannot* be assumed to be the preeminent good for most individuals within our society, the difficulties above afford no reason for denying that good of participation to those who choose to regard it as as a central value. And again, the good of democratic political life cannot be realized unless political power is distributed on the basis of participation and persuasive ability alone. When wealth or other extraneous factors distort the allocation of political power, political debate becomes merely a conflict of particular interests, not an attempt to persuade others to revise their understanding of social goods in the light of shared values. A weaker communitarian view that identifies participation as *an* important good therefore overlaps with the traditional liberal justifications for establishing the fair value of political liberties. Liberals can argue for a guarantee of the fair value of the political liberties as the best means, within a framework of rights, for representing individuals equally and protecting them from the abuse of power. Communitarians can add that we must protect the political sphere because "when politics goes well, we can know a good in common that we cannot know alone."[16]

This kind of justification also improves upon the Walzer's view of politics. Walzer sometimes suggests that once we have located all other goods within their proper spheres and secured their autonomy, politics will consist merely in policing this set of preestablished boundaries. This view is clearly inadequate, however, since, as Walzer also recognizes, politics not only protects the boundaries between different distributive contexts but redraws them as well. Moreover, there is a tension between Walzer's commitment to democracy and his commitment to letting the community decide matters for itself, since the community may choose undemocratic policies. If politics can redefine the boundaries between different social goods, what is to prevent a political redefinition of the social meaning of politics itself, so that it becomes legitimate to distribute political power on the basis of wealth, for example? With this redefinition, however, the idea of keeping the distribution of goods autonomous, that is, Walzer's idea of "complex equality," would vanish. In order to preserve the ideal of complex equality, then, our understanding of the meaning of democratic politics is crucial. Our view of politics must function like a gyroscope, stabilizing the idea of complex equality by stabilizing itself. The view above does explain why the equation of politics with democracy is stable, in two different ways. First, if the strong communitarian position is correct, citizens will find the experience of democratic debate self-reinforcing. The greater our experience of genuine democratic discussion, the more we will want to protect the independence of such discussion. Second, even if democratic debate is only important to *some* citizens, this weaker justification reinforces other, more traditional justifications for insuring that political power is kept free of the influence of other goods. On either account, our understanding of the appropriate principle for the distribution of political power should be relatively resistant to change.

We arrive, then, at two formulations of the same view. On the communitarian formulation, "democracy . . . is *the political way* of allocating power. Every extrinsic reason is ruled out. What counts is argument among the citizens. Democracy puts a premium on speech, persuasion and rhetorical skill."[17] On the liberal formulation, "When we consider the distinctive role of the political process in determining the laws and policies that apply to the basic structure, it is not implausible that these liberties alone should receive the special guarantee of fair-value."[18] The guiding idea is the same: individuals are entitled to exercise power on the basis of participation and persuasive abilities alone. And this principle applies no matter how many participate, that is, to both representative and participatory democracy.

While indifferent to the extent of participation, however, this conception of politics may have some rather sweeping redistributive implications. Throughout this book, I have argued against the idea of overall equality, and by implication, against the idea of simple equality within and across "spheres of justice." Nevertheless, a limited but potentially powerful kind of argument for simple equality does emerge here. For given certain empirical conditions, the ideal of complex equality may itself require a greater degree of simple equality than Walzer believes. For example, greater equalization of income within the sphere of the market may ultimately be the only feasible way of achieving the goal of insulating the distribution of goods, particularly political power, from the power of money. Thus, a large degree of simple equality within the sphere of the market may have an instrumental justification from both the liberal and communitarian perspective.

Nevertheless, there is a difference between how liberals and communitarians approach this question, at least so far as the liberal position is represented by Rawls. Rawls has argued against a "wider guarantee" of the equal worth of political liberty, that is, against a more equal distribution of other goods such as income, on the basis that a guarantee of this sort "is either irrational or superfluous or socially divisive" given the difference principle.[19] Since I have argued that the difference principle relies on empirical generalizations that are too sweeping and uncertain, this solution is not open to us. We have no choice but to deal with the problem of providing a wider guarantee for the political liberties directly. In other words, we must deal directly with the problems involved in the public financing and regulation of campaign contributions, the control of bureaucratic power, and the issues of representation and reapportionment. We must also directly address a wide variety of questions about the empirical relationships that exist between wealth and power, while recognizing that these questions are and must be highly controversial given the current findings of social science.

This is yet another area in which we cannot expect a philosophical resolution of our difficulties. We cannot avoid this sort of controversy by moving to a higher level of abstraction. Without reference to empirical generalizations about the effects of various property rights on our ability to exercise our basic liberties, for example, it would seem impossible to settle "the general form and content" of those liberties in advance, as Rawls suggests. It bears repeating, however, that our empirical investigations should be guided by the question of how much simple equality is necessary to insulate politics from the power of other goods, not by the aim of establishing simple equality itself. Distributing power equally within the political sphere, for example, would deny the principle that power should be distributed differentially on the basis of participation and persuasion alone. And of course our goal cannot be to redistribute goods so that political power becomes one element in an index, or formula, for making groups equal or well-off. As I have already argued, that goal is meaningless.

Community

Within the framework sketched above, social justice must be largely a matter of "complex equality." This is so not only because, as Walzer remarks, we already live in a society in which the social meanings of various goods have become distinct, but also because, as I have shown, there is no intelligible and workable metric for commensurating those goods. And although there is controversy about the extent to which shared social meanings are available within our culture, Walzer's arguments would seem to show that we can appeal to a great number of collective understandings in settling questions of distributive justice. But of course, problems remain.

When members of a community differ among themselves about how to balance principles of justice, Walzer's approach offers no overall guidance. Such advice would defeat the whole rationale of his account, which is to leave these questions to communal decision. But in the absence of a common tradition, disagreements about how to draw the boundaries between different distributive contexts and their appropriate principles may prove quite intractable. In our own society, for example, there is considerable disagreement about whether health care belongs in the sphere of communal provision or in the sphere of the market. In cases like this, it seems we must appeal to standards that transcend shared understandings. As Dworkin remarks, "if justice is only a matter of following shared understandings, then how can the parties be debating about justice when there is no shared understanding? In this situation, no solution can *possibly* be just."[20] At this point, we return to the controversy that opened this book. For in response to this criticism, Walzer has obstinately refused to draw any precise lines between spheres of justice, insisting that boundary disputes can seldom if ever be settled once and for all,[21] and, according to Dworkin, this refusal shows why we must continue to theorize about social justice in a more abstract way.

Where social meanings are in dispute, however, communitarians do try to provide arguments that show why it is more appropriate to assign particular goods to one sphere of justice rather than another, so we should look more closely at the sort of arguments they make. Concerning this problem of boundary disputes, Dworkin maintains that Walzer actually relies on a "hidden premise": "He tacitly assumes that there are only a limited number of spheres of justice whose essential principles have been established in advance and must therefore remain the same for all societies. He also assumes that though any particular community is free to choose whether to assign some type of resource to one or another of these fixed spheres, by developing the appropriate conventions, it must do so on an all-or-nothing basis."[22] Unfortunately, this interpretation of Walzer's argument is flatly contradicted by his discussions of many distributive problems. For example, Walzer argues that education should be distributed in our own society partly as a matter of need (the sphere of communal welfare), partly as a matter of desert or qualification (the sphere of office) and partly as a matter of entitlement (the market).[23] But whether or not his criticisms rest on an accurate reading of Walzer's theory, Dworkin's claim that there is "hidden premise" is correct, although he misidentifies it. The more or less hidden premise of all communitarian writers is that, whenever possible, we should distribute goods in a way that strengthens community. Dworkin makes the right criticism of Walzer, but then draws the wrong conclusion. When traditional understandings of justice come into radical conflict, this does not mean that we are unable to carry moral argument any further, as both Dworkin and Walzer appear to believe. Instead, the topic of debate shifts. We must now ask whether a proposed distribution might strengthen our sense of community and whether a heightened sense of community is desirable or not.

The way in which communitarians use the term "community" is not always clear, however. For example, communitarians sometimes appear to argue that we should strengthen community by expanding the sphere of need or communal provision, as when Walzer argues the case for a national health care system.[24] In appealing to the value of community in this context, Walzer seems to be appealing to the value of a sense of belonging or emotional affiliation. And his thought seems to be that where membership includes more goods, individuals will develop a more inclusive sense of membership. At other times, however, communitarians argue that we can strengthen community by expanding participation, not provision. Here an appeal to community is really an appeal to the values of the particular participatory ideal of association discussed earlier.

While a sense of belonging or fraternity is an important good, it is problematic whether we should appeal to it in trying to find a further standard for resolving disagreements about justice. "Community" in this first sense is something that can be manufactured in a number of objectionable ways, such as indoctrination, and it often increases intolerance toward outsiders. On the second understanding of community, however, we are united not simply by a sense of belonging, but by emotional ties to a democratic way of life that itself encourages the airing and toleration of differences. Typically, this ideal suggests that we should broaden democratic participation in politics and also that we should democratize other spheres of justice, like the schools and the workplace, in order to increase discussion about the way in which goods like education and work should be distributed in nonpolitical contexts. In other words, we should simultaneously broaden participation in government and decentralize the decisions that government makes.

This more specific ideal of community does give us a further standard to appeal to in justifying distributive policies, both with respect to the distribution of decision-making power itself and with respect to the resources that allow individuals to participate. However, this ideal cannot resolve all of our difficulties, since disagreement about justice is apt to be replaced by disagreement about the value of democratic community itself.

Consider, for example, people who find collective provision too expensive and collective judgment too intrusive. They may not wish to feel more deeply "connected" to this community, nor may they wish to be constantly "engaged" in debate. Of course, the kind of democratic participation described earlier promises to transform these attitudes, so that collective decisions are no longer *experienced* in these ways. But the people in question may doubt both the transformative power of such debate in the first place, and the desirability of such a transformation in any event. They might still prefer that commodities, education, health care, and so on, be distributed for separate reasons and may continue to hope that the distribution of one good does not pattern, or dominate the distribution of any other. But they prefer this plurality without the additional aim of encouraging discussion or engagement: they value having distinct spheres of distribution because this plurality protects them *from* the sort of collective judgments that would follow if every area of life were "democratized."[25]

Of course, these hypothetical people represent the liberal view, since liberalism assumes that "there are many conflicting and incommensurable conceptions of the good, each compatible with the autonomy and rationality of human persons."[26] Since actual political debate must involve conflict over different conceptions of our (final) good, the liberal assumes that such debate *must* break down at some point and that collective judgment must be experienced as intrusive. The liberal strategy is therefore to try to skirt this possibility. Instead of recommending actual political debate, liberals try to formulate a view of persons and of goods in abstraction from our disagreements. The more abstract our formulation, the less we favor any one conception of the good and therefore the better our chance of reaching consensus. As we have seen in earlier chapters, however, the irony of this strategy is that as our theory becomes more and more abstract we becomes less and less able to answer any actual questions about distribution. In the end, we may be able to agree on the importance of a few basic rights, but even this agreement lacks content and does no more than constrain our decisions in an extremely broad way. But as communitarians emphasize, and as commonsense pluralism also insists, it is precisely in being able to answer detailed questions that we give the notion of "social justice" some meaning (or not).

In place of a hypothetical, philosophical procedure for reaching agreement, then, communitarians suggest that we use an actual, political one. This actual procedure does not leave persons as they are while determining the distribution of goods, but engages and changes persons in the process of determining such distributions. And since this is a procedural solution, there is no guarantee that the requisite transformation will take place: discussion may break down for all of the reasons that liberals have advanced. In this light, an actual procedure has only one thing that can be said for it: while hypothetical procedures apparently *cannot* produce the necessary agreement, political procedures *may*. This is less than a ringing endorsement of the communitarian ideal, and it suggests that we treat the notion of democratic community with a great deal of circumspection. Nevertheless, this ideal does furnish an additional standard when current views of justice deadlock. Moreover, it explicitly recognizes and indeed incorporates the force of Dworkin's complaint about Walzer: "Walzer's idea of complex equality . . . ignores the 'social meaning' of a tradition much more fundamental than the discrete traditions it asks us to respect. For it is part of *our common political life*, if anything is, that justice is our critic not our mirror, that any decision about the distribution of any good . . . may be reopened no matter how firm the traditions that are then challenged, that we may always ask of some settled institutional scheme whether it is fair."[27] In this context, Dworkin's invocation of a common political life is somewhat inappropriate, since what Dworkin really wishes to do is to reopen a discussion of justice among philosophers. But Dworkin's view that distributive questions should be constantly open to discussion is correct, and the participatory ideal described earlier attempts to do just that.

In response to the charge that a more political approach to questions of justice is dangerous and vague, then, let us review our findings: First, as we have seen in earlier chapters, the alternative philosophical approach to questions of social justice apparently cannot work. Second, there are nevertheless several strong arguments in favor of both a framework of basic rights and a certain understanding of politics. This common ground shows that a political approach to social justice does not entail that anything goes. Third, within a political framework, we can appeal to the extant social meanings of different kinds of goods in order to resolve a fairly large number of distributive questions. Fourth, when this method breaks down, we can argue that wherever possible we should favor distributions that strengthen community, both in the sense of psychological connectedness and, more importantly, in the sense of a particular participatory ideal of association. That ideal holds out at least the promise that we can create an understanding of justice where none was before. As we saw in Chapter 6, this is also the promise of "Kantian constructivism." The difference, however, is that in this case the promise is to be realized through actual political debate rather than philosophical argument.

Of course, once all of these alternatives have been tried we may still fail to agree. And we might still complain that, "in this situation, no solution can *possibly* be just."[28] But what, finally, is the matter with that? As always, the question is whether we should reject a theory of justice because it is imprecise, or reject the implicit standard of precision that would justify such a rejection. But in this context, the idea that there must be an answer to every distributive question appears to be a kind of dogma. It may even be true, as Irving Kristol has said, that "in the same way as men cannot for long tolerate a sense of spiritual meaninglessness in their individual lives, so they cannot for long accept a society in which power, privilege, and property are not distributed according to some morally meaningful criteria."[29] This is simply a truism, however, which says nothing at all about what a morally meaningful criterion might be. Our task has been to try to answer that prior question.

Finally, a note of warning is in order. As we saw in Chapter 6, Rawls's theory is motivated by a deep desire to reach agreement. To this end, even the essential task of political philosophy has been redefined, so that it is now understood to be practical rather than epistemological in character. As we also saw in Chapter 6, Rawls's desire to achieve a certain level of agreement leads him to propose principles of justice that are implausibly rigid, even though Rawls's objectives are already more modest than the other theorists of justice whose work we have examined. Communitarians, as we have seen, entertain a similar project of "creating" agreement and it is fueled by the same desire. As Nancy Rosenblum has observed of Walzer, "The most obvious reason for wanting a community of shared meanings is dislike of disagreement."[30] But having rejected one approach to the topic of social justice, we should now be wary of rushing to embrace the idea of democratic community as a new solution to all of our difficulties, particularly if we are motivated simply by a desire to agree. It makes a difference whether our attempt to generate agreement begins from existing disagreements or whether it simply abstracts from those disagreements as if they were not there. Still, democratic debate may also fail to create agreement. Moreover, while communitarians have historically been attracted to the ideal of agreement between citizens, it is something of a historical aberration for liberals to be as taken with that ideal as they recently have been. Instead, liberals have usually agreed to disagree. And liberals have traditionally emphasized the fallibility of *philosophical* reason as well as the ineliminable character of political conflict. In any case, the basic civil and political liberties traditionally favored by liberals presuppose such conflict. Those liberties cannot be effective unless individuals constantly exercise and, in so doing, clarify and reassert those liberties in practice. If conflicts over the more particular requirements of justice persist, then, it should not be thought that something is necessarily amiss, either with ourselves, or with a theoretical account of justice that fails to resolve all conflicts for us.

Future Prospects

Throughout this book my concern has been with the degree of precision it is appropriate to expect from a theory of social justice, on the assumption that a discussion of this question might restore a sense of the importance of politics within the field of political philosophy. On the basis of previous chapters, then, let me review briefly the set of problems that still face any attempt to provide an account of justice that goes beyond a plurality of commonsense principles.

First, any theory of social justice that tries to provide standards for redressing the overall situation of each member of society must find some coherent and practicable way of distinguishing the natural, social, and personal factors that together presumably determine what individuals are capable of claiming. Of the many obvious difficulties with this theory, I will note only the most salient: (1) the impossibility of distinguishing between the holdings that have been acquired by actual members of society and the holdings that might have been acquired in another society or a "state of nature"; (2) the impossibility of establishing the counterfactual claims necessary to justify policies of direct compensation to individuals for discrimination or unfairness occurring any time in a more or less remote past; (3) the necessity of nevertheless rectifying the cumulative effects of individual transactions, both free and fraudulent; (4) the impossibility of regarding market demand as an objective measure of the worth of individual contributions, together with the impossibility of commensurating the value of most goods and services at all except through the operation of markets; (5) the conceptual and practical difficulty of assessing welfare, developmental or otherwise; and (6) the requirement that principles of justice nevertheless allow reasonable economic efficiency and political stability.

All of these problems must be addressed. In the sort of theory we are now reviewing, they must be dealt with in a way that is fair to each and every person directly. But if we consider all of these difficulties together, it would appear that in order to realize social justice on a case by case basis we would have to keep track of "an endless variety of circumstances, transactions, and changing relative positions."[31] Or, as Rawls puts the matter in *A Theory of Justice*: "If it is asked in the abstract whether one distribution of a given stock of things to individuals with known desires and preferences is better than another, then there simply is no answer to this question."[32]

Of course, conservative critics of the idea of social justice have long maintained that there is little sense to abstract questions about what particular individuals should receive. In order to underscore the way in which Rawls's approach to the question of social justice is novel, I have emphasized that he accepts this conservative critique and tries to shift our attention to the basic structure. But while we might be persuaded to ignore the claims of individuals to some extent for the sake of achieving a workable theory of social justice, Rawls's theory purchases clarity at too great a cost to our intuitions about individual justice. And we cannot make justice as fairness more sensitive to the claims of definite individuals without reintroducing the complexities and balancing problems that Rawls hopes to avoid. Nor can we simply waive the problem of special needs, as Rawls has tried to do, and postpone the problem of constructing an index for normal healthy individuals. Indeed, to postpone the indexing problem is to admit that there is no definite solution to the problem of social justice in these terms.

But further, it is not clear that Rawls's later revisions of justice as fairness really give us any reason for preferring his two principles. Even if we accept the priority of liberty, which now follows almost by definition from Rawls's conception of the person, we may still prefer some other, less definite principle for organizing social and economic institutions. Indeed, the parties in the original position cannot make a clear choice without more information about how the institutions of a well-ordered society are likely to work in practice. Unless we can predict the results produced by different basic structures, Rawls's strategy of leaving individual shares to pure procedural justice will not work. But we cannot reliably predict the results produced by social institutions even under conditions of full information. This problem, together with the difficulty of constructing an index, make the idea of coordinating all of our basic institutions from a single perspective unfeasible. Moreover, even Rawls's argument for the priority of liberty fails unless we accept the question-begging stipulation that liberty has priority only under "reasonably favorable" circumstances.

Finally, as we saw in Chapters 5 and 6, neither Douglas Rae's principle of "simple justice" nor the notion of a "distribution-sensitive consequentialism" solves the problem of balancing first principles; instead they express that problem. In order to satisfy transitivity requirements, these moral conceptions ask us to choose between overall combinations of equality and aggregate welfare. And as Rawls observes, not only are these principles "too abstract and comprehensive" for us to have any confidence in our judgment, but "there are enormous complications in interpreting what they mean." As I showed in Chapter 6, the only way of avoiding these difficulties is Rawls's strategy of relying on a theory of institutions for the basic structure as a whole. With the failure of that solution, we must look for less abstract and comprehensive principles whose requirements we can actually understand.

By process of elimination, then, we come back to the ideas of "complex equality" and "commonsense pluralism." Pluralism breaks down the problem of social justice into smaller, more manageable questions about what should happen in the economy, the family, the schools, and in politics. The fact that pluralism transfers many supposedly philosophical questions about social justice back to politics is not, properly speaking, the end of this discussion, but the beginning of another. If the argument of this book is correct, most problems of social justice can only be resolved politically; this follows from the very limited sort of theoretical precision that the subject matter of social justice permits. But although this is the only solution for most distributive problems, even this solution will fail if politics degenerates into nothing more than a conflict between particular interests. As Walzer points out, the ultimate appeal in conflicts over justice is "not to particular interests, or even to a public interest conceived as their sum, but to collective values."[33] Where politics is nothing more than a conflict between particular interests, social justice can only emerge by accident. There is, then, a procedural aspect even to the idea of complex equality. For we must make certain that our institutions encourage disinterested debate, good-faith disagreement, wise practical judgment, and truly communal decision. As I argued above, these are primarily questions about strengthening democratic community within the framework of rights discussed above.

Since these questions are not my major concern, I will confine myself to three observations. First, there is no mystery about the sort of institutional reforms that might strengthen a sense of democratic community. The most obvious include political decentralization, the creation and expansion of "town-hall" associations, an expansion of the referendum process and other forms of "common work and common doing."[34] The purpose of these reforms is of course to overcome the problems of scale, complexity, and parochialism mentioned above in discussing the strong communitarian position. Political philosophers and political scientists now need to take a more serious look at such proposals, since their practical feasibility not only determines the attractiveness of this ideal of community but also sets limits on the extent to which we can hope to create a more precise political definition of justice by means of this ideal. To evaluate the feasibility of these sorts of proposals, however, political philosophers must rely more heavily on historical analysis and empirical policy studies than they generally have in the past.

Second, thinking about these kinds of proposals involves a theoretical shift of focus away from distributive questions. Of course, many of these reforms do involve redistributing both decision-making power and, to a certain extent, other sorts of goods that may distort democratic debate. Nevertheless, we should now be primarily concerned with thinking about a new form of politics, one that involves a different conception of community and a different attitude toward debate and conflict, not with devising a definite redistributive program that will somehow guarantee that a new politics will emerge. Redistributive issues, then, should become secondary, and theorists should instead turn to the problem of institutional changes that might encourage a stronger sense of political possibility.

Finally, we need to address not only the practical problems confronting the strong communitarian position, but some of the conceptual ones as well. As noted above, the most important of these is the tendency of communitarian theorists to run together the ideas of freedom and autonomy (and in some instances, to conflate the latter with a specific understanding of "virtue"). This conflation is objectionable because it gives the impression that an attempt is being made to conceal the imposition of communal standards by misrepresenting such imposition as a form of liberation. This impression unnecessarily tends to confirm the suspicion that the communitarian position is dangerous. Freedom and autonomy are distinct values: practices that protect freedom may interfere with the development of autonomy and attempts to make agents more autonomous may entail significant restrictions on their freedom. One can therefore understand why liberals legitimately worry about threats to freedom justified on the basis of autonomy, particularly when politics is envisioned as a school for autonomy and virtue. But in fact conceptual distinctions between freedom, autonomy, and virtue say nothing about which value we should prefer in cases of conflict, nor do they establish what sort of society is best suited to promoting one value or the other. As Richard Flathman observes, we might prefer communitarian arrangements on the basis of freedom if we think that such arrangements actually reduce obstacles to action and thereby enhance agency. Or we might prefer more individualistic arrangements on the basis of autonomy, if we think that autonomy flourishes best where communal standards are weak.[35] We must make such distinctions in the first place, however, if we are to begin to think more clearly about the question of how much community is desirable. Once we do, our attention should shift away from a minute examination of the rules of distribution to a more complex set of questions about the degree and kind of association we want.

Happily, these questions go beyond the scope of this book and do not need to be taken up here. The only remaining task is to forestall one possible misinterpretation of my argument. I have argued that social justice is a vague and indefinite idea, and it might be thought that this conclusion really supports the views of conservative skeptics like Oakeshott, and particularly Hayek, who find the idea meaningless. I believe that Hayek's view is in fact correct, if we suppose that social justice must be what Dworkin, Ackerman, and so many other recent theorists have assumed it to be, namely, a precise set of distributive patterns which must be constantly reestablished. I believe Hayek's conclusion is also correct if society is presently what both he and pessimistic communitarians like MacIntyre generally suppose it to be, namely, nothing more than an aggregation of individuals who have no common understandings or collective values at all. But from the perspective of this book, both sides make the same mistake. The only difference between Hayek and those he attacks is that Hayek correctly assumes that the project undertaken by most of the theorists examined in this book cannot be carried through successfully. What we should reject, however, is not the idea of social justice itself, but a misconceived standard of precision that both sides share, a standard which leads to absurdly hypothetical and complex accounts of social justice on the one hand, and to complete dismissal on the other. Neither response is appropriate to the subject matter.

My argument opened with an epigraph from Aristotle's *Ethics*. I close with Aristotle's cautionary remarks about the study of politics, drawn from the same passage of the *Ethics*:

> Now fine and just actions, which political science investigates, admit of much variety and fluctuation of opinion, so that they might be thought to exist only by convention, and not by nature. And goods also give rise to a similar fluctuation because they bring harm to many people; for before now men have been undone by reason of their wealth, and others by reason of their courage. We must be content, then, in speaking

about such subjects and with such assumptions to indicate the truth roughly and in outline . . . for it is the mark of an educated man to look for precision in each class of things just so far as the subject admits.[36]

Reading the current literature on social justice one cannot help thinking that we are "uneducated" in Aristotle's sense of the word. Most contemporary accounts of social justice are extremely abstract and counterfactual. They ignore the inevitable indeterminacy of their subject matter and deny the role of politics in providing answers where philosophy cannot. But we cannot simply appeal to the practical judgment of the educated man, as Aristotle does, in order to show that most recent theories of justice demand too much precision from their subject matter. If we could be easily satisfied with Aristotle's appeal to the educated man, we would not have witnessed the sustained effort of so many for so long to provide an impossibly exact and systematic theory of social justice. For this reason, I have been forced to take a longer road to Aristotle's conclusion.

NOTES

1. Walzer, *Spheres of Justice*, p. 8.
2. Ibid., p. 70.
3. Sandel, *Liberalism and the Limits of Justice*, p. 5.
4. For this version of the communitarian position, see MacIntyre, *After Virtue*, p. 67.
5. Walzer, *Spheres of Justice*, p. xv.
6. For an example of the strong liberal response, see Thigpen and Downing, "Liberalism and the Communitarian Critique," p. 646. For a more extended discussion of Walzer, also see Thigpen and Downing, "Beyond Shared Understandings," p. 451-73.
7. See Gutmann, "Communitarian Critics of Liberalism," p. 315.
8. MacIntyre, *After Virtue*, p. 42 (emphasis added).
9. For a representative selection of critical articles on the project of deducing human rights from the idea of rational agency, see *Human Rights: Nomos 23*, ed. Pennock and Chapman. In this context, the article by Richard Friedman is particularly relevant, since it illustrates why Rawls has abandoned the strong liberal position. According to Friedman, theorists like Gewirth want to show that a rational agent must claim certain basic rights on prudential grounds. But Friedman argues that a rational agent *must* base his right-claim on prudential grounds only if refusing to claim such a right would contradict his character as an agent *and* it would also be self-contradictory for him to claim that right on some other basis, such as desert or merit. However, Gewirth never shows why the latter basis for claiming rights is also self-contradictory. In other words, Gewirth *presupposes* the egalitarian view that eliminates desert

and other kinds of considerations as bases for claiming rights. Of course, the view that agents should possess equal rights is something Gewirth set out to *demonstrate*. Rawls, however, simply begins with this assumption, as I point out below in the text. See Friedman, "The Basis of Human Rights: A Critique of Gewirth's Theory," pp. 148-58.

10. For an exploration of this confusion, see Taylor, "The Nature and Scope of Distributive Justice," pp. 34-50.

11. At an even deeper level, we might object in principle to Rawls's practical aim of 'settling' the question of the priority of liberty. Why is it desirable to have a philosophical justification for the priority of liberty that cuts off discussion of the priority of liberty for some unspecified length of time? In at least one view of liberalism, a liberal society should not grant any principle this sort of protection. For further discussion of these issues, see Flathman, *The Philosophy and Politics of Freedom*, pp. 269-78, 299-302.

12. It might be objected that what my argument shows is not that the philosopher and the citizen are asking different kinds of questions but that the kind of question traditionally asked by the philosopher makes no sense. In other words, philosophers are under an illusion if they think that the sort of knowledge they are pursuing belongs to a different realm than that of the citizen. If the philosopher is asking for a neutral political theory, utterly unconditioned by his own historical situation and political commitments, then I agree that he is an impossible character. But Rawls and many other liberal theorists would also agree that a completely "unsituated" political theory is impossible. When I contrast citizens and philosophers, then, it is in the context of my discussion of liberal theory. The contrast is between citizens who are concerned with justifying basic civil and political liberties on the basis of full information about present circumstances and liberal theorists who wish to justify a similar set of liberties without such knowledge and in advance of changes in circumstance.

13. Barber, *Strong Democracy*, p. 190.

14. For a discussion of these problems, see ibid., particularly pp. 262-63.

15. Hirsch expresses this last worry in "The Threnody of Liberalism," p. 426.

16. Sandel, *Liberalism and the Limits of Justice*, p. 183. This understanding of politics receives some additional support from perfectionist theories of justice. Given William Galston's recent criticisms of Walzer, this claim may seem surprising (see Galston's review of *Spheres of Justice* in *Ethics*, 94, no. 2 [1984]: 329-33). But it all depends on what kind of perfectionism we are considering. As Galston notes, Walzer rejects the Platonic view that political power should be distributed on the basis of special political knowledge. But of course, Aristotle also rejects the Platonic view, in part because it denies the good of full political membership to citizens. Galston's own rather Aristotelian theory of justice balances the "internal claims" of self-development against the "external

claims" of the community's need for excellence in leadership. But those external claims must be modified by a prudential concern about the abuse of power. The question is whether we can design some imperfect practical procedure for reliably distinguishing the sophist from the statesman, both of whom have great persuasive ability. Where extended debate and participation are the best imperfect procedures for selecting leaders who understand the detailed requirements of the political sphere, the positions of Walzer and Galston come to the same thing, practically speaking. In other words, Walzer's principle for distributing political power will have an additional, instrumental justification in terms of its tendency to select those who do have "special knowledge" of a particular political kind.

17. Walzer, *Spheres of Justice*, p. 303.

18. Rawls, "The Basic Liberties and Their Priority," p. 43.

19. Ibid., p. 44.

20. Dworkin, "To Each His Own," p. 3.

21. In reply to these criticisms, Walzer has invoked Dworkin's own theory of judicial interpretation as a model of how we should try to interpret the social meaning of various goods. ("'Spheres of Justice': An Exchange," *New York Review of Books*, July 21, 1983, p. 44.) An appraisal of this particular line of response would take us too far afield, especially in light of the book-length discussions recently published by each theorist on the theme of interpretation. Rather than follow Walzer at this point, I develop a different response to Dworkin in the text.

22. Dworkin, "To Each His Own," p. 6.

23. Walzer, "Spheres of Justice," pp. 201, 209, 218.

24. Ibid., pp. 84-91.

25. This sort of objection is in Rosenblum's review of *Spheres of Justice,* "Moral Membership in a Postliberal State," pp. 590-94.

26. Rawls, "Social Unity and Primary Goods," p. 160.

27. Dworkin, "To Each His Own," p. 6.

28. Dworkin, "To Each His Own," p. 5.

29. This is Kristol's response to Hayek's argument that we should prefer a "free" to a "just" society on the grounds that, while we may know what freedom is, we cannot know what "social justice" means. "When Virtue Loses All Her Loveliness," p. 97.

30. Rosenblum, "Moral Membership in a Postliberal State," p. 595.

31. Rawls, *A Theory of Justice*, p. 90.

32. Ibid., p. 88.

33. Walzer, *Spheres of Justice*, p. 82.

34. For a detailed list of proposals, see Barber, *Strong Democracy*, pp. 261-313.

35. Flathman, *The Philosophy and Politics of Freedom*, p. 121.

36. Aristotle, *Nicomachean Ethics*, p. 936.

Bibliography

Ackerman, Bruce A. *Social Justice in the Liberal State.* New Haven: Yale University Press, 1980.
————. "What Is Neutral about Neutrality?" *Ethics*, 93, no. 2 (1983): 372-90.
Aristotle, *Nichomachean Ethics.* Ed. Richard McKeon, *The Basic Works of Aristotle.* New York: Random House, 1941.
Arrow, Kenneth. "Some Ordinalist-Utilitarian Notes on Rawls' Theory of Justice." *The Journal of Philosophy*, 70, no. 9 (1973): 245-63.
Arthur, John and William Shaw, eds. *Justice and Economic Distribution.* Englewood Cliffs, N.J.: Prentice-Hall, 1978.
Barber, Benjamin. "Justifying Justice: Problems of Psychology, Politics, and Measurement in Rawls." *The American Political Science Review*, 69 (1975): 663-74.
————. *Strong Democracy.* Berkeley: University of California Press, 1984.
————. "Unconstrained Conversations." *Ethics*, 93, no. 2 (1983): 330-48.
Barry, Brian. "John Rawls and the Priority of Liberty." *Philosophy and Public Affairs*, 2 (1973): 274-90.
————. *The Liberal Theory of Justice.* Oxford: Clarendon Press, 1973.
Beauchamp, Tom L. "Distributive Justice and the Difference Principle." *John Rawls' Theory of Justice.* Eds. H. Gene Blocker and Elizabeth Smith. Athens: Ohio University Press, 1980, 132-62.
Bedau, Hugo. "Social Justice and Social Institutions." *Midwest Studies in Philosophy*, Vol. 5. Ed. Peter French. Minneapolis: University of Minnesota Press, 1980, 159-76.
Bell, Daniel. "On Meritocracy and Equality." *The Public Interest*, no. 29 (1972): 26-69.
Bennet, John. "Ethics and Markets." *Philosophy and Public Affairs*, 14, no. 2 (1985): 195-205.
Blocker, H. Gene and Elizabeth Smith, eds. *John Rawls' Theory of Justice.* Athens: Ohio University Press, 1980.
Bloom, Allan. "Justice: John Rawls vs. the Tradition of Political Philosophy." *The American Political Science Review*, 69 (1975): 648-62.
Bowie, Norman. "Some Comments on Rawls' Theory of Justice." *Social Theory and Practice*, 3, no. 1 (1974): 65-74.
————. *Towards a New Theory of Distributive Justice.* Amherst: University of Massachusetts Press, 1971.
Buchanan, Allen E. *Marx and Justice.* Totowa, N.J.: Rowman and Littlefield, 1982.

Daniels, Norman. "Equal Liberty and Unequal Worth of Liberty." *Reading Rawls*. Ed. Norman Daniels. New York: Basic Books, 1975, 253-81.

———. "Health Care Needs and Distributive Justice." *Philosophy and Public Affairs*, 10, no. 2 (1981): 146-80.

———. "Meritocracy." *Justice and Economic Distribution*. Eds. John Arthur and William Shaw. Englewood Cliffs, N.J.: Prentice-Hall, 1978.

———. "Moral Theory and the Plasticity of Persons." *The Monist*, 62, no. 3 (1979): 265-87.

———. *Reading Rawls: Critical Studies of a Theory of Justice*. New York: Basic Books, 1975.

———. "Reflective Equilibrium and Archimedean Points." *Canadian Journal of Philosophy*, 10, no. 1 (1980): 82-103.

———. "Wide Reflective Equilibrium and Theory Acceptance in Ethics." *Journal of Philosophy*, 76 (1979): 256-82.

Darwall, Stephen. "A Defense of the Kantian Interpretation." *Ethics*, 86, no. 2 (1976): 164-70.

Delaney, C. F. "Rawls on Method." *Canadian Journal of Philosophy*, supp. vol. 3 (1977): 153-61.

di Quattro, Arthur. "Rawls and Left Criticism." *Political Theory*, 2, no. 1 (1983): 53-78.

Dworkin, Ronald. "To Each His Own." *The New York Review of Books*, April 14, 1983, pp. 4-6.

———. "Liberalism." *Public and Private Mortality*. Ed. Stuart Hampshire. Cambridge: Cambridge University Press, 1978.

———. "The Original Position." *Reading Rawls*. Ed. Norman Daniels. New York: Basic Books, 1974.

———. *Taking Rights Seriously*. Cambridge: Harvard University Press, 1978.

———. "What Is Equality? Part One: Equality of Welfare." *Philosophy and Public Affairs*, 10, no. 3 (1981): 283-346.

———. "What Is Equality? Part Two: Equality of Resources." *Philosophy and Public Affairs*, 10, no. 4 (1981): 283-345.

———. "What Liberalism Isn't." *The New York Review of Books*, January 20, 1983, 47-50.

———. "Why Liberals Should Believe in Equality." *The New York Review of Books*, February 3, 1983, 32-34.

Feinberg, Joel. *Doing and Deserving*. Princeton: Princeton University Press, 1970.

———. "Rawls and Intuitionism." *Reading Rawls*. Ed. Norman Daniels. New York: Basic Books, 1975, 108-23.

Finnis, John. *Natural Law and Natural Rights*. Oxford: Clarendon Press, 1980.

Fishkin, James. "Can There Be a Neutral Theory of Justice?" *Ethics*, 93, no. 2 (1983): 348-57.

———. *Justice, Equal Opportunity and the Family*. New Haven: Yale University Press, 1983.

———. "Justice and Rationality: Some Objections to the Central Argument in Rawls' Theory." *The American Political Science Review*, 69 (1973): 615-29.

———. *Tyranny and Legitimacy: A Critique of Political Theories.* Baltimore: Johns Hopkins University Press, 1979.

Flathman, Richard. "Egalitarian Blood and Skeptical Turnips." *Ethics,* 93, no. 2 (1983): 357-67.

———. "Equality and Generalization: A Formal Analysis." *Nomos 9: Equality.* Eds. J. R. Pennock and John W. Chapman. New York: Atherton, 1967.

———. *The Philosophy and Politics of Freedom.* Chicago: University of Chicago Press, 1987.

———. *The Practice of Rights.* Cambridge: Cambridge University Press, 1976.

Fried, Charles. *Right and Wrong.* Cambridge: Harvard University Press, 1978.

Friedman, M. "Choice, Chance and the Personal Distribution of Income." *Journal of Political Economy,* 61 (1953): 277-99.

Friedman, Richard. "The Basis of Rights: A Critique of Gewirth's Theory." *Nomos 23: Human Rights.* Eds. J. R. Pennock and John W. Chapman. New York: Atherton, 1981.

Fullwinder, Robert K. "Review of *Justice and the Human Good.*" *Ethics,* 93, no. 1 (1982): 157-60.

Galston, William. "Defending Liberalism." *The American Political Science Review,* 76, no. 3 (1982): 621-29.

———. *Justice and the Human Good.* Chicago: University of Chicago Press, 1980.

———. "Moral Personality and Liberal Theory." *Political Theory,* 10, no. 4 (1982): 492-519.

Gauthier, David. "Justice and Natural Endowment: Toward a Critique of Rawls' Ideological Framework." *Social Theory and Practice,* 3, no. 1 (1974): 3-26.

Goldman, Holly Smith. "Rawls and Utilitarianism." *John Rawls' Theory of Justice.* Eds. H. Gene Blocker and Elizabeth Smith. Athens: Ohio University Press (1980): 346-95.

Gordon, Scott. "John Rawls' Difference Principle, Utilitarianism, and the Optimum Degree of Inequality." *The Journal of Philosophy,* 70, no. 9 (1973): 275-80.

Gutmann, Amy. "Communitarian Critics of Liberalism." *Philosophy and Public Affairs,* 14, no. 3 (1985): 308-22.

———. *Liberal Equality.* Cambridge: Cambridge University Press, 1980.

Harsanyi, John C. "Can the Maximin Principle Serve as a Basis for Morality? A Critique of John Rawls' Theory." *The American Political Science Review,* 69 (1975): 594-606.

Hart, H. L. A. "Between Utility and Rights." *Columbia Law Review,* 79 (1981): 828-46.

———. "Rawls on Liberty and Its Priority." *Reading Rawls.* Ed. Norman Daniels. New York: Basic Books, 1974, 230-52.

———. "Are There Any Natural Rights?" *Philosophical Review,* 64 (1955): 175-91.

Hayek, Friedrich A. *The Mirage of Social Justice,* Vol. 2 of *Law, Legislation and Liberty.* London: Routledge and Kegan Paul, 1976.

Hirsch, H. N. "The Threnody of Liberalism." *Political Theory,* 14, no. 3 (1986): 423-51.

Jencks, Christopher, Marshall Smith, Henry Arland, Mary Jo Bane, David Cohen, Herbert Gintis, Barbara Heyns, and Stephen Michelson. *Inequality: A Reassessment of the Effect of Family and Schooling in America.* New York: Basic Books, 1972.

Johnson, Oliver A. "Autonomy in Kant and Rawls: A Reply to Stephen Darwall's 'A Defense of the Kantian Interpretation'." *Ethics,* 87 (1977): 251-54.

———. "Heteronomy and Autonomy: Rawls and Kant." *Midwest Studies in Philosphy,* 2 (1977): 277-79.

Kristol, Irving. "When Virtue Loses All Her Loveliness." *The Democratic Idea in America.* New York: Harper Torchbooks, 1972.

Levine, Andrew. "Rawls' Kantianism." *Social Theory and Practice,* 3 (1974): 47-63.

Litan, Robert. "On Rectification in Nozick's Minimal State." *Political Theory,* 5, no. 2 (1977): 233-47.

Lyons, David. "The Nature and Soundness of the Contract and Coherence Arguments." *Reading Rawls.* Ed. Norman Daniels. New York: Basic Books, 1975, 141-67.

MacIntyre, Alasdair. *After Virtue.* Notre Dame: University of Notre Dame Press, 1981.

———. *Against the Self-Images of the Age.* Notre Dame: University of Notre Dame Press, 1978.

Mackie, J. L. "Competitors in Conversation." *The Times Literary Supplement,* no. 3, 190 (April 17, 1981): 443.

Macleod, A. M. "Critical Notice: Rawls' Theory of Justice." *Dialogue: Canadian Philosophical Review,* 13 (1974): 139-59.

Michelman, Frank I. "In Pursuit of Constitutional Welfare Rights: One View of Rawls' Theory of Justice." *The University of Pennsylvania Law Review,* 121 (1972-73): 962-1019.

Miller, David. *Social Justice.* Oxford: Clarendon Press, 1976.

Miner, Jacob. *Schooling, Experience and Earnings.* New York: National Bureau of Economic Research, 1974.

Nagel, Thomas. "Equality." *Mortal Questions.* Cambridge: Cambridge University Press, 1979, 1-16.

Narvenson, Jan. "Rawls and Utilitarianism." *The Limits of Utilitarianism.* Ed. Harlan B. Miller. Minneapolis: University of Minnesota Press, 1982, 128-41.

Nielsen, Kai. "Our Considered Judgments." *Ratio,* 19 (1977): 39-46.

Nielsen, Kai and Roger Shiner, eds. *New Essays in Contract Theory. Canadian Journal of Philosophy,* supp. vol. 3 (1977).

Nietzsche, Friedrich. *Schopenhauer as Educator.* Trans. James Hillesheim. Chicago: Henry Regnery Company, 1965.

Norton, David L. *Personal Destinies: A Philosophy of Ethical Individualism.* Princeton: Princeton University Press, 1976.

Nozick, Robert. *Anarchy, State, and Utopia.* New York: Basic Books, 1974.

———. "Moral Complications and Moral Structures." *Natural Law Forum,* 13 (1969): 1-50.

Pogge, T. M. W. *Kant, Rawls and Global Justice.* Unpublished Ph.D. dissertation, Harvard University, 1983.

Rae, Douglas. "A Principle of Simple Justice." *Philosophy, Politics and Society, Fifth Series.* Ed. James Fishkin and Peter Laslett. London: Blackwell, 1979, 134-54.

———. "Maximin Justice and an Alternative Principle of General Advantage." *The American Political Science Review,* 69 (1975): 630-47.

Rawls, John. "The Basic Liberties and Their Priority." *The Tanner Lectures on Human Values.* Ed. Sterling McMurrin. Salt Lake City: University of Utah Press, 1982, 1-88. Delivered at the University of Michigan, April 10, 1981.

———. "The Basic Structure as Subject." *Values and Morals.* Ed. A. Goldman and J. Kim. Dordrecht: D. Reidel, 1978, 47-73.

———. "Constitutional Liberty and the Concept of Justice." *Nomos VI: Justice.* Ed. C. J. Friedrich and John W. Chapman. New York: Atherton, 1963, 98-125.

———. "Fairness to Goodness." *The Philosophical Review,* 84 (1975): 536-34.

———. "The Independence of Moral Theory." *Proceedings and Addresses of the American Philosophical Association,* 48 (1975): 5-22. Presidential Address to the American Philosophical Association, Eastern Division, 1974.

———. "Justice as Fairness." *The Journal of Philosophy,* 54 (1957): 653-62.

———. "Justice as Fairness: Political, Not Metaphysical." *Philosophy and Public Affairs,* 14, no. 4 (1985): 223-52.

———. "Justice as Reciprocity." *Utilitarianism.* Ed. Samuel Gorovitz. New York: Bobbs-Merrill Co., 1971, 242-68.

———. "A Kantian Conception of Equality." *Cambridge Review,* Feb. (1975): 94-99.

———. "Kantian Constructivism in Moral Theory." *The Journal of Philosophy,* 77 (1980): 515-72.

———. "Legal Obligation and the Duty of Fair Play." *Law and Philosophy,* 77 (1980): 515-72.

———. "Reply to Alexander Musgrave." *The Quarterly Journal of Economics,* 88 (1974): 633-55.

———. "Reply to Lyons and Teitelman." *The Journal of Philosophy,* 69 (1972): 556-57.

———. "Social Unity and Primary Goods." *Utilitarianism and Beyond.* Eds. Amartya Sen and Bernard Williams. Cambridge: Cambridge University Press, 1982, 159-87.

———. "Some Reasons for the Maximin Criterion." *American Economic Review,* 64 (1974): 141-46.

———. *A Theory of Justice.* Cambridge: Harvard University Press, 1971.

———. "Two Concepts of Rules." *The Philosophical Review,* 64 (1955): 3-32.

Rescher, Nicholas. *Distributive Justice.* New York: Bobbs-Merrill, 1966.

Rosenblum, Nancy. "Moral Membership in a Postliberal State." *World Politics*, 36 (1984): 555-96.

Ross, W. D. *The Right and the Good*. Oxford: Clarendon Press, 1930.

Rousseau, Jean-Jacques. *The Social Contract*. Trans. Maurice Cranston. New York: Penguin Books, 1968.

Runciman, W. G. *Relative Deprivation and Social Justice*. Berkeley: University of California Press, 1966.

Sandel, Michael J. *Liberalism and the Limits of Justice*. Cambridge: Cambridge University Press, 1982.

Scanlon, T. M. "Contractualism and Utilitarianism." *Utilitarianism and Beyond*. Eds. Amartya Sen and Bernard Williams. Cambridge: Cambridge University Press, 1982, 103-29.

——. "Nozick on Rights, Liberty, and Property." *Philosophy and Public Affairs*, 6 (1976): 3-25.

——. "Preference and Urgency." *Journal of Philosophy*, 72 (1975): 655-69.

——. "Rawls' Theory of Justice." *The University of Pennsylvania Law Review*, 121 (1972-73): 1020-69.

——. "Rights, Goals, and Fairness." *Public and Private Morality*. Ed. Stuart Hampshire. Cambridge: Cambridge University Press, 1978, 93-113.

Scheffler, Samuel. "Moral Skepticism and Ideals of the Person." *The Monist*, 62 (1979): 288-303.

——. *The Rejection of Consequentialism*. Oxford: Clarendon Press, 1982.

Schweickert, David. "Should Rawls Be a Socialist?" *Social Theory and Practice*, 5, no. 1 (1978): 1-29.

Sen, Amartya, and Bernard Williams, eds. *Utilitarianism and Beyond*. Cambridge: Cambridge University Press, 1982.

Sher, George. "Effort, Ability, and Personal Desert." *Philosophy and Public Affairs*, 8, no. 4 (1979): 361-76.

Shue, Henry. "The Current Fashions: Trickle Downs by Arrow and Close-Knits by Rawls." *The Journal of Philosophy*, 71 (1974): 319-27.

Simmons, A. John. *Moral Principles and Political Obligations*. Princeton: Princeton University Press, 1979.

Singer, Marcus G. "Justice, Theory, and a Theory of Justice." *Philosophy of Science*, 44 (1977): 594-617.

Singer, Peter. "Sidgwick and Reflective Equilibrium." *The Monist*, 58 (1974): 490-517.

Slote, Michael. "Desert, Consent, and Justice." *Philosophy and Public Affairs*, 2, no. 4 (1973): 323-47.

Smart, J. J. C., and Bernard Williams, eds. *Utilitarianism: For and Against*. Cambridge: Cambridge University Press, 1973.

Smith, M. B. E. "Rawls and Intuitionism." *New Essays on Contract Theory*. Eds. Kai Nielsen and Roger Shiner. *Canadian Journal of Philosophy*, supp. vol. 3 (1977): 163-78.

Sterba, James. "Justice as Desert." *Social Theory and Practice*, 3, no. 1 (1974): 101-16.

Strasnick, Steven. Review of *Understanding Rawls* by Robert Paul Wolff. *Journal of Philosophy*, 81 (1979): 506-10.

Taylor, Charles. "Interpretation and the Sciences of Man." Eds. Fred Dallmayer and Thomas McCarthy. *Understanding Social Inquiry*. Notre Dame: University of Notre Dame Press, 1977, 101-31.

————. "The Nature and Scope of Distributive Justice." *Philosophy and the Human Sciences: Philosophical Papers 2*. Cambridge: Cambridge University Press, 1985.

Thigpen, Robert, and Lyle Downing. "Beyond Shared Understandings." *Political Theory*, 14, no. 3 (1986): 451-73.

————. "Liberalism and the Communitarian Critique." *American Journal of Political Science*, 31, no. 4 (1987): 637-56.

Thurow, Lester. "Toward a Definition of Economic Justice." *The Public Interest*, 31 (1973): 56-81.

Walzer, Michael. *Spheres of Justice*. New York: Basic Books, 1983.

————. " 'Spheres of Justice': An Exchange." *The New York Review of Books*, July 21, 1983, 43-46.

Williams, Bernard A. O. "A Critique of Utilitarianism." *Utilitarianism: For and Against*. Eds. J. J. C. Smart and Bernard Williams. Cambridge: Cambridge University Press, 1973.

————. "The Idea of Equality." *Philosophy, Politics and Society: Second Series*. Eds. P. Laslett and W. G. Runciman. New York: Barnes and Noble, 1962.

————. "Persons, Character and Morality." *The Identities of Persons*. Ed. A. Rorty. Berkeley: University of California Press, 1981, 197-216.

————. "Space Talk: The Conversation Continued." *Ethics*, 93, no. 2 (1983): 367-72.

Wolff, Robert Paul. *Understanding Rawls*. Princeton: Princeton University Press, 1977.

Wood, A. "The Marxian Critique of Justice." *Philosophy and Public Affairs*, 1, no. 3 (1972): 244-82.

Index

Note on the Author

DAVID MAPEL is assistant professor of political science at the University of Colorado at Boulder. He has a master's degree from the London School of Economics and a master's degree and doctorate from Johns Hopkins University. This is his first book.